SYDNEY
& Surrounds
A DISCOVERY GUIDE

Photography by Steve Parish

Text by Robert James Wallace

Steve Parish
PUBLISHING

www.steveparish.com.au

Contents

The Big Picture   8–13

Sydney City   14–31

Sydney Suburbs   32–53

Greater Sydney   54–75

North of Sydney

West of Sydney

South of Sydney

ACT

Introduction

Whenever I am fortunate enough to travel around the Greater Sydney region, I find myself continually overwhelmed by two things — the spectacular natural environs and the tremendous sense of history and heritage that pervades the cities and towns. Sydney has proudly accepted its place alongside the world's great cities, and justifiably so. It has become a role model for post-modern culture, famous for its sunshine, sea, fashion, arts, cuisine, extravagant festivals and multicultural tolerance. It is no surprise that millions of visitors from all over the world are attracted to this lively and engaging town.

When I turned eighteen, I moved to Sydney to train as a diver with the Royal Australian Navy. Together with friends from The New South Wales Underwater Research Group, I spent much of my free time exploring and photographing the watery realms around Sydney Harbour and the heads. Here I discovered incredibly rich natural environments teeming with life. Not long after I was transferred to Jervis Bay and continued my obsession with underwater photography. This eventually evolved into a desire to capture as much of Australia's nature, people and places as possible.

For a photographer like myself, the contrast between Sydney's old buildings and its modern structures provides a fantastic source of social photography. From the iconic, triangulated shells of the Sydney Opera House to the elegant, Romanesque lines of the Queen Victoria Building, there is always an intriguing range of architectural styles to capture. This is also true of the towns surrounding Sydney, many of which contain vivid relics from Australia's colonial and Indigenous past.

Outside Sydney, the opportunities to capture the State's natural environment are endless. New South Wales is blessed with a superb coastline, vast areas of national park, snow-capped mountains, desert plains and pristine marine habitats. The scenery is sensational. Within these places exist some of Australia's most fascinating native animals: colourful parrots, secretive Platypuses and inquisitive dolphins among many other species. They all make compelling subjects for my photographs.

With every new visit, I realise still how much more there is to discover in New South Wales. It is a State full of opportunities and adventures and, with this in mind, my guide has been designed to embrace every traveller's need for flexibility. Whether you intend to use this book as a basis for exciting daytrips, weekends or for embarking on more extensive driving tours of the region, I hope you feel the same sense of excitement and anticipation that I always feel on my trips around Sydney and its beautiful surrounds.

Left, top to bottom: Steve Parish has photographed Australia's cities and landscapes for over 40 years; AXA Building next to the Museum of Contemporary Art; The Rocks; The Three Sisters, Blue Mountains National Park. *Opposite:* George Street.

How to Use this Book

This book has been designed with all readers in mind, whether domestic daytrippers wanting to explore — or escape — the city, or international travellers planning a more extensive tour around Sydney and the surrounding region. Simple-to-follow maps, tried-and-tested driving tours, interesting snippets of local and natural history, as well as lists of "Things to See and Do", make this book one of the most straightforward guides to what you can expect to see on your travels throughout Greater Sydney. Local authors have covered almost every kilometre of this vast region, so you can be sure that this guide recommends the best that Sydney and its surrounds have to offer. Marvel at the natural scenery and wildlife or enjoy the city's cultural attractions. Most of all, enjoy your stay!

Region-by-Region Format

This guide is split into seven sections with the pages throughout colour-coded by region. Each section contains a full-page map, on which the major towns, attractions, national parks and driving tours along highways and byways are indicated. In each of the seven regions — Sydney City, Sydney Suburbs, Greater Sydney, North of Sydney, West of Sydney, South of Sydney and the ACT — you'll be introduced to the area's history, geography and major industries. Also covered are national parks and flora and fauna, as well as information regarding a region's cultural and ecological significance. This region-by-region format leads from the State's vibrant and cultural capital, Sydney, to the wilderness of Blue Mountains National Park in the west and Royal National Park in the south. To the north lies Newcastle, hub of the Lower Hunter. Of course, rather than being distinct entities, these regions overlap and merge, so wherever possible the driving tours and maps within this guide venture into the boundaries of adjoining regions to explain the easiest way to travel from one area of New South Wales to the next.

Natural History Breakout Boxes

From the Hunter Valley to the Southern Highlands, New South Wales features stunning wilderness areas: reserves, national parks and marine parks all teeming with unique kinds of flora and fauna. Even the parklands of Sydney, its harbour and leafy suburbs are home to all sorts of mammals, birds and reptiles, which keen-eyed visitors can readily observe. The breakout boxes scattered throughout this book explain the natural history of a particular area, giving you a sneak preview of the different species you can expect to see and the best places to see them.

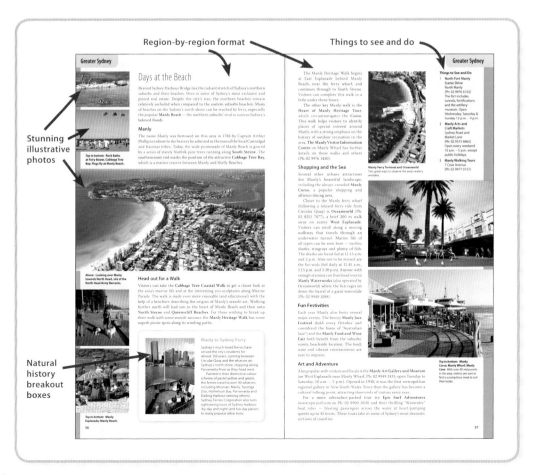

Location, Location, Location

For convenience, the location or contact details of rangers' stations, tourist sites and advisory bodies are listed in the text in each chapter or in the Things to See and Do column on the relevant spread.

How to Use the Maps

Consistent, easy-to-read maps highlight the major destinations and the best tours discussed within each section. Use the map in each chapter to locate these attractions, which are highlighted in pink. The maps have been designed to display most of the major places of interest mentioned in the text.

Above: **Hampden Bridge, Kangaroo Valley** Greater Sydney provides a history-rich, scenic driving experience. *Bottom right:* **Gordons Bay.**

Things to See and Do

Every State of Australia has its own character and provides visitors with a number of natural and artificial surprises. Listed in the Things to See and Do section of all Steve Parish Discovery Guides are the top activities for travellers wanting to make the most of their trip. Whether visiting bustling markets, absorbing city culture, attending annual festivals or visiting theme parks, this section gives you the low-down on the area's not-to-be-missed activities and shares information like where to get the best view of incredible natural formations.

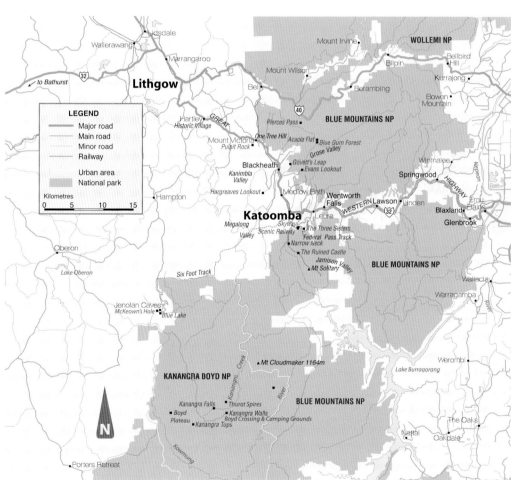

Dramatic Driving Tours

New South Wales is a huge State and every twist and turn of the road renews the landscape and presents a different vista to appreciate from your car window. This guide takes you on a tour from Sydney to the ACT to the Hunter Valley, following the most spectacularly scenic routes. Use the instructive text, with the maps as back-up, to wind your way over the region's highways and byways, stopping at the best lookouts, picnic areas, tourist sites, nature reserves and historic sites, all via the State's most charming townships and cities.

The Big Picture

Blue Mountains An excursion to this exceptional wilderness is a must for any visit to Sydney.

Terrigal is a popular Central Coast getaway with sensational surf beaches.

Sydney Opera House The famous icon is a perennial favourite of Sydney visitors.

Budderoo National Park is just one of the many spectacular natural areas in the Illawarra region.

As Australia's oldest and most populous State, New South Wales is a region thoroughly traversed by the footsteps of many visitors through many different time periods. Its historical and cultural nerve centre, Sydney, has matured into a truly international city that is a focal point of Australian tourism. Intrepid travellers will find themselves introduced to a State of fascinating character and endless diversity should they choose to venture beyond the city's bounds.

Greater Sydney comprises a spectrum of travel destinations that includes the Australian Capital Territory and the nation's capital, Canberra. Consequently, visitors may be spoilt for choice in the number of great places to see. A good start includes two excellent national parks located within 30 km of Sydney's CBD: Ku-ring-gai Chase and Royal. Further north is the Hunter Valley and Newcastle, with its communal vibe and sparkling beaches. The main attraction of this area is its wineries, which are world-class. To Sydney's south are the Southern Highlands (NSW's own slice of England) and the Illawarra region, dotted with picturesque

Historic George St The heritage buildings shown here remain a feature of this busy street.

coastal towns and spectacular areas of wilderness. To the west of Sydney lie the Blue Mountains: a must-see destination for any visitor to the area.

Colonisation to Settlement

New South Wales was named in 1770 after British explorer James Cook navigated the east coast of Australia. Due to London's overcrowded prisons, the British government decided to establish a penal colony around Cook's original landing site at Botany Bay. In 1788, with more than 700 convicts in tow, the First Fleet arrived in Sydney and commenced settlement under the leadership of Governor Arthur Phillip. The colony endured incredible hardships, but by the early 19th century Sydney was showing signs of civilisation and exploration of its wider surrounds began.

Agriculture to Industry

The crossing of the Blue Mountains in 1813 opened up the land to ambitious graziers and, with the discovery of gold in the 1850s, dramatically altered the social and economic landscape of the State. At the same time, England's Industrial Revolution was generating a healthy demand for raw materials, thus securing future prosperity for both New South Wales and Australia.

Aboriginal Settlement

Although they are not related to any known South-East Asian race, Aborigines are thought to have migrated from that area between 40–50,000 years ago. Around 3000 Aborigines are estimated to have been living in the Sydney region at the time of its "discovery". Living a simple and sustainable tribal existence, Aborigines had little need for technological advancement, but developed complex and cultural societies.

20th Century to Present

Following Australia's federation in 1901, New South Wales became a State and, several years later, Canberra became the nation's capital. Riding a great wave of economic expansion, Sydney's population approached one million people. Recovering from the Depression, the Harbour Bridge opened in 1932 and the years after World War II saw both increasing immigration and huge growth west of Sydney. The Opera House opened in 1973 and boom times continued throughout the 1980s. In 1988, Sydney revelled in bicentennial celebrations that provided an exciting precursor to its main event. Using the global stage of the 2000 Olympic Games, Sydney created an unforgettable impression on the new millennium. Today, Sydney continues its rise as a progressive and cosmopolitan city.

Above: **The 2000 Sydney Olympic Games** caught the eye of the world and enhanced Sydney's reputation as a global city. *Below, top to bottom:* **Coastal Cliff Walk, South Head; Maroubra Beach** Sydney's magnificent harbour and beaches are key attractions for both residents and visitors.

A Brief History of Sydney and Surrounds

1770 — Lieutenant James Cook (later Captain Cook) lands at Botany Bay.

1788 — The First Fleet arrives and creates a settlement at Port Jackson.

1813 — Blaxland, Wentworth and Lawson cross the Blue Mountains, beginning an era of Australian exploration.

1840 — All convict transportation to New South Wales is abolished.

1851 — Gold is discovered in Bathurst.

1901 — Australia becomes a federation; New South Wales becomes a State.

1911 — The Australian Capital Territory is formed and Canberra becomes the new national capital.

Delights for the Visitor

Whether you are an inexhaustible shopaholic, wilderness explorer, wine connoisseur, budget backpacker, or casual tourist, Sydney and its surrounds are guaranteed to satisfy your most particular leisure needs. From bustling and trendy cities to laid-back coastal towns, from snow-capped mountains to subtropical rainforest, the region offers its visitors endless pastimes: culinary odysseys, skiing holidays, nature trails, seaside retreats and urban adventures.

Geology, Topography and Climate

New South Wales encompasses a vast area of land — over 800,000 km² — that is generally divided into four distinct geographical regions. The State's dominant geological feature is the Great Dividing Range, which runs the entire length of the State and separates these regions from each other. The highest parts of the range are the alpine regions in the State's south, which include Mt Kosciuszko, the highest mountain in the country. The western slopes of the Great Dividing Range slip into fertile valleys and farmland. This important agricultural belt gradually tapers out westward to flat, ceaseless plains punctuated by remote and dusty outposts brimming with typical outback character. The eastern side of the range is steeper. Here are the lush, forested tablelands and plateaus (places like the magnificent Blue Mountains), which descend into the most populated stretches of the State: the New South Wales coast. The State is watered by mighty rivers, such as the Darling and Murray, and their tributaries: the Lachlan and Murrumbidgee rivers in the State's south.

The many environments surrounding Sydney make for a wide range of climates. Generally, the further north you travel, the warmer it becomes. It is hotter (and much drier) out west than it is on the coast. The mountains are cooler and receive more rainfall than the lower regions. Sydney itself has a temperate climate, with warm summers and cool winters. Its maritime location makes rainfall somewhat unpredictable. Average temperatures in Sydney during summer (November to January) are between 25.8–17.1 °C with mean winter temperatures (June to August) between 17.3–7.2 °C. Canberra is subject to more extreme conditions, with hot summers and frosty winters. Rainfall is evenly distributed throughout the year. Canberra's average summer temperatures are between 27.6–13.1 °C with mean winter temperatures between 12.4–0.9 °C.

Rainforest

The rainforest found around Sydney can be categorised as temperate (either cool or warm), dry, littoral, or subtropical. Despite its ecological importance, much of this rainforest has been cleared and most remaining areas are protected by national parks. It usually exists in small, isolated patches at reasonably high altitudes and requires high rainfall and fertile soils. Pockets can be found in the Blue Mountains, Budderoo (*left*), Morton, and Royal National Parks.

The Magnificent Coast

Since Captain Arthur Phillip declared Port Jackson one of the finest harbours in the world, Sydney's residents and its visitors have shown an unwavering devotion to its coastline. Sydney's metropolitan beaches are some of the finest in the country and are a staple of urban recreation. To the north and south of Sydney are some truly spectacular coastal environments — sandstone bluffs, rocky headlands, inlets, bays, and endless tracts of white sand and blue water. This is just the surface. Marine parks such as Jervis Bay provide a haven for all kinds of underwater life.

Bondi Beach Sydney's (and possibly Australia's) most famous beach has earned its reputation partly because of its convenient and trendy location, but mostly because of its undeniable beauty. The water is crystalline, the waves are great for surfing, and the beach is flanked at each end by stunning sandstone headlands — a favourite of overseas visitors and eastern suburbs locals.

Gerringong is part of the Illawarra Coast to the south of Sydney and typical of the seaside towns in this area. It is graced with expansive beaches and a backdrop of green, rolling hills.

Port Stephens is a magnificent sheltered bay on New South Wales' Lower North Coast. Well known for its boating, fishing and dolphins, it is a popular retreat for Sydney and Newcastle residents.

Marvellous Mountains

Below, left to right: Kanangra–Boyd National Park; Wollemi National Park.

The heart of the Great Dividing Range intersects New South Wales and some of the most spectacular highland regions in the country lie along this vast and imposing stretch of mountains. In a geographical sense, these mountains "divide" the rivers and streams that flow eastwards into the Pacific Ocean from those that drain westwards into the Murray–Darling Basin. The highest areas of the range are known as the Australian Alps and include the iconic Snowy Mountains, which lie south of Canberra. The highest peak in the country, Mt Kosciuszko, rises to 2228 m. Perhaps the most famous mountainous area in the Greater Sydney region lies within Blue Mountains National Park to the city's west. Despite its name, this national park is actually a rugged sandstone plateau. It is always a memorable place to visit, with incredible scenery, forested slopes, and abundant wildlife.

Numerous National Parks

For sheer diversity of natural environments, few Australian States can match New South Wales. From the snow-capped peaks of the high country to the sparkling blue waters of the coast, Sydney and its surrounds provide nature lovers and outdoor adventurers with a spectacular array of national parks. Some of these parks are World-Heritage-listed areas (such as Blue Mountains National Park) containing flora and fauna unique to Australia. Most preserve a strong Aboriginal heritage, featuring important Indigenous sites and artefacts.

City dwellers need not travel far to experience real wilderness. There are a number of superb national parks located within the boundary of Sydney's metropolitan area — Lane Cove, Ku-ring-gai Chase, Royal and Sydney Harbour National Parks. Take a visit to any of these parks and you will be immediately impressed by the abundance of wildlife and number of different habitats in such close proximity to a city of more than four million people.

In any direction beyond the city's reach, but still within close range, are some truly exceptional national parks — Thirlmere Lakes, Brisbane Water, Wollemi and the Blue Mountains: the shining centerpiece among Greater Sydney's hefty trove of natural treasures.

Bouddi National Park This pristine wilderness is approximately 95 km north of Sydney. It comprises some 1500 ha of eucalypt woodlands, coastal heath and sandstone bluffs, and incorporates a 300 ha marine park around picturesque Maitland Bay. Like many national parks in the Greater Sydney region, Bouddi has a strong Aboriginal heritage and there are numerous areas in the park for examining Indigenous art and artefacts.

Royal National Park Australia's first national park (gazetted in 1879) is less than an hour's drive from the centre of Sydney. It has extensive walking tracks, swimming areas and camping sites.

Chinese Garden, Darling Harbour.

Outside Lowenbrau Keller, The Rocks One of Sydney's best Bavarian brasseries.

Sydney's Gay and Lesbian Mardi Gras has earned itself a world-famous reputation.

Sydney's City to Surf Race attracts thousands of local and international competitors.

Culture and Celebration

Sydney loves to party. Its hardworking population takes plenty of time out to enjoy a number of major events throughout the year. The themes for these occasions are wide and varied: food, art, music, culture, sport, history and heritage all provide a basis for festive celebration. Mixed in with the city's marquee events are many regional festivals, which, although lacking the city's glitz and glamour, are just as spirited and full of local colour.

In the City

Wild thunderstorms generate only some of the electricity in Sydney's atmosphere over summer. The fireworks extravaganza of New Year's Eve ignites the festival fuse for the year. The epitome of the city's flair and sophistication is the **Sydney Festival**, Australia's largest cultural event, which creates a month-long buzz that culminates in **Australia Day** celebrations on 26 January. The **Big Day Out**, held on this day and featuring a huge collection of local and international acts, is the pinnacle of Australian music festivals. Also on this day is the **Survival Festival**, the Aboriginal version of Australia Day. **Chinese New Year** celebrations (featuring Darling Harbour's Dragon Boat Races) are in full swing soon after and are followed in early March by the jubilant flamboyance of Sydney's world-famous **Gay and Lesbian Mardi Gras**. A week before Good Friday the Sydney Showground comes alive with twelve days of entertainment at the **Royal Easter Show**. The winter months see the **Sydney Film Festival** previewing short and feature-length films from many different countries. There are also numerous arts, crafts, books and antique festivals during this time. August features the legendary **City to Surf** foot race, which then leads into spring and racing of another kind when Royal Randwick and Rosehill Gardens host the country's premier horse-racing action. Sport features heavily during September, when the annual rugby league and union grand finals are played. Spring is also the season for The Royal Botanic Gardens **Spring Festival**, which delights visitors with its exhilarating displays of floral ingenuity.

Outside Sydney

Of the hundreds of different festivals and events held in the towns and cities outside Sydney every year, livestock and farming shows are a popular diversion. Kiama, in the Illawarra region, hosts its **Agricultural Show** in January and the nation's capital is busy hosting the **Royal Show**, **Canberra Festival**, and **National Folk Festival** during February and March.

Cultural Stews and Melting Pots

Right, top to bottom: Sydney is home to people of all colours, creeds and cultures; Cabramatta is a lively suburb with a large Vietnamese community.

As one of the world's most cosmopolitan cities, Sydney plays host to a vibrant and fascinating mix of multicultural events throughout the year.

Among the more popular celebrations are the annual **St Patrick's Day** parade and Chinese New Year festivities held around the CBD. The **Greek Festival** of Sydney, an extended and joyous celebration of Hellenic culture, occurs during March and April. A touch of exotic mystery runs throughout **Loy Krathong**, the traditional celebration of Thai culture held in Parramatta. This "water festival" features thousands of candles, incense and tiny boats floating freely along the river.

Canberra celebrates its cultural blend during the annual **National Multicultural Festival** — an extravaganza of food, music, theatre, dance and exhibitions.

Also during March, the Hunter Valley showcases an exciting range of food and wines during its **Annual Harvest Festival**. The mood then changes somewhat for the more sombre celebrations of **Anzac Day** (commemorating the landing of Anzac troops at Gallipoli in 1915), which have special significance at the Australian War Memorial in Canberra. In August, Newcastle enlivens visitors with its traditional **Jazz Festival** and the Blue Mountains celebrate a chilly (if not white) mid-year Christmas during **Yulefest**. Spring is the time for spectacular floral events, including Canberra's own visually stunning **Floriade** festival and the Southern Highlands' **Tulip Time**, another revered occasion for flower enthusiasts. The lead up to Christmas is a bustling time for all, each town marking the season in its own distinctive style.

Above: **Floriade** is Canberra's celebration of spring and one of the nation's most distinguished floral festivals.

Below: **Sydney to Hobart Yacht Race** This great ocean race is one of the city's glamour events and heralds the beginning of a new sporting year.

Bottom right: **Telstra Stadium** The main arena of the 2000 Olympics is now a multi-purpose venue that hosts rugby league, union, cricket and Australian rules games as well as major international concerts.

Further Information

Sydney Visitor Centre
Cnr Argyle & Playfair St,
The Rocks, Sydney
(Ph: 02 9240 8788)

Canberra and Region Visitors Centre
330 Northbourne Av,
Dickson, ACT
(Ph: 1300 554 114)

Wollongong Visitor Information Centre
93 Crown St
(Ph: 1800 240 737)

Newcastle Visitor Information Centre
361 Hunter St
(Ph: 1800 654 588)

Dept Environment and Conservation (NSW)
(Ph: 02 9995 5000)

Roads and Traffic Authority (NSW)
(Ph: 13 2701)

Sporting Spectacles

Sydney is the birthplace of Australian sport and is home to magnificent sporting arenas, including Sydney Olympic Stadium (the primary venue for the 2000 Olympics) and Rosehill Gardens (home of the prestigious Golden Slipper horse race). Rugby union, league and cricket showcase regular international fixtures. Traditionally a southern sport, "Aussie rules" has also enjoyed rampant popularity since the Sydney Swans claimed their inaugural title in 2005.

Sydney City

Silver
Gull

It is little wonder that Sydney, with a population of 4.5 million, is often mistaken for Australia's capital. Home to many of the nation's most recognisable tourism icons — Bondi Beach, Sydney Opera House, the Harbour Bridge and Sydney Tower — the city also contains some of Australia's oldest buildings and historical artefacts. Sydney is the initial destination for millions of overseas visitors, with Australia's international gateway airport, Kingsford Smith, situated close to historic Botany Bay. Sydney's residents are proud of their energetic hometown, its "global city" reputation and brassy, fast-paced lifestyle. The city, built by Sydney Harbour, is Australia's main port and a thriving economic and entrepreneurial powerhouse. As a centre for entertainment, finance, education, sport, culture and tourism, present-day Sydney has something for everyone.

From Humble Beginnings to Modern Prosperity

It didn't take long for British explorer James Cook and the First Fleet of 1788 to recognise the potential of this sun-drenched location on Australia's eastern coastline. The city was founded as a penal colony and named after Viscount Sydney, patron of Captain Cook. Years of hardship followed, but in less than 200 years the city was transformed from a harsh Georgian labour camp to a thriving metropolis. The northernmost stretch of George Street, one of Sydney CBD's most bustling thoroughfares, was quickly constructed and is now Australia's oldest roadway. It runs through the historic Rocks district and links the present-day CBD with Circular Quay, the Harbour Bridge and the Sydney Harbour foreshore.

Gold discoveries west of Sydney in the 1850s brought an influx of immigrants in search of fortune. The city boomed and although the gold reserves did not last, they generated enormous wealth. Sydney had 500,000 inhabitants at the beginning of the 20th century, making it one of the largest cities in the western world at that time.

Following World War II, and throughout the latter half of the 20th century, Sydney experienced rapid development. Its international reputation steadily grew in the 1980s thanks to a series of headline-grabbing achievements. Australia's upset win in the America's Cup yacht race, Paul Hogan's *Crocodile Dundee* flicks, Hollywood's adoption of Mel Gibson, and the popular tunes of AC/DC, INXS, Midnight Oil and Olivia Newton John, among others, helped garner recognition for the nation's talent.

Top to bottom: **Sydney Tower; Darling Harbour; Royal Botanic Gardens; Sydney Hospital.**

Sydney's iconic Opera House and Harbour Bridge are a highlight of any visit to Sydney Year round these spectacular feats of architecture are the focus of sightseers and tourists. Whether you enjoy the majestic concert halls of the Opera House or the breathtaking views that the Harbour Bridge offers, both will leave you awe-struck.

Sydney Today

In the 21st century, Sydney has had further opportunity to develop its flair. The phenomenally successful 2000 Olympics, and Australia's high medal count, not only confirmed the Aussie love of sport and personal endeavour but also proved that Sydney loves a party and is capable of hosting major events in a friendly and efficient manner. Today, visitors can see hundreds of years of history and growth, as well as modern art spaces and a plethora of world-class sport and entertainment venues confined within an area small enough for anyone to explore on a self-paced walking tour. Sydney attracts more than two million international visitors a year and it is not hard to see why. Today, Sydney offers a multitude of activities — its shining star continues to rise.

Above, top to bottom: **Harbour Ferry; City Bus tours** The city's ferries and the modern River Cat and Jet Cat boats take visitors to North Sydney and the northern beaches such as Manly. Buses, including tour buses, provide the most extensive public transportation.

Further Information

Sydney Visitor Centre
Cnr Argyle and Playfair Sts,
The Rocks
(Ph: 02 9240 8788)
33 Wheat Rd, Darling
Harbour
(Ph: 02 9240 8788)
www.sydneyvisitorcentre.com

Transport Infoline
(Bus, train, ferry information)
(Ph: 13 1500)
www.131500.com.au

Tourism Australia
201 Sussex Street,
Sydney
(Ph: 02 9361 1338)
www.tourism.australia.com

Tourism NSW
66 Harrington Street
The Rocks
(Ph: 02 9931 1111)
www.tourism.nsw.gov.au

Clockwise from top left: **Darling Harbour; The monorail crosses Pyrmont Bridge; Sydney Harbour Bridge; Anzac Bridge** The many bridges offer not only access across the harbour but also the opportunity to see how glorious the city looks from some spectacular vantage points.

Getting Around

Those intent on seeing the city on foot will be aided by wide footpaths and the **City Gateways** public works program that links the town centre with busy nearby suburbs such as Darlinghurst, Kings Cross and Broadway. For the less energetic, metropolitan Sydney is well served by the **City Circle** trains that pass through the CBD, from Central Railway and Broadway to Circular Quay and The Rocks. Trains generally run from 5 a.m. – midnight and provide access to western and southern Sydney. The overhead **Sydney Monorail** service, somewhat shunned by locals but popular with visitors, serves Chinatown, George Street and Darling Harbour. **CountryLink** trains operate for journeys further afield.

A series of underground **Cross City Tunnels** help motorists avoid the snare of CBD traffic, but bridges from Pyrmont Bridge and Anzac Bridge, to the world-famous "coathanger" (Sydney Harbour Bridge) act as the city's main arteries for vehicular traffic.

Above: **Railway line linking King Cross and Sydney City** Public transport options are many and varied in Sydney. Visitors can travel to most areas via road, rail or water.

Sydney Heritage

By the Harbour

The bottom right corner shows the Sydney Harbour Bridge (2) leading into the CBD from North Sydney. To the left is The Rocks (4) and Circular Quay (3) with the CBD beyond. Left again is the Opera House (1), Government House (9), Parliament House, The Mint and State Library (5) and Woolloomooloo Bay (8) seen here behind Farm Cove, which runs from Mrs Macquaries Point (extreme left, just out of view) around the Farm Cove foreshores of the Royal Botanic Gardens to the Sydney Opera House.

Amid the modern glass and steel constructions that are Sydney's towering skyscrapers there are many notable, long-standing buildings that portray the historic aspects of Sydney's character. Some, such as the **Great Synagogue** opposite Hyde Park, **St Stephen's Cathedral,** opened in 1935 in Macquarie Street, and the truly weathered **St George's Church** in Castlereagh Street, hemmed-in and overshadowed as they are by newly constructed neighbours, are still striking examples of heritage architecture. Other long-standing Sydney buildings, such as the massive **QVB (Queen Victoria Building,** once housing a concert hall and the city library) and **St Mary's Cathedral** (which, when the final spire was completed in 2000, took 179 years to build), dominate their surroundings due to their sheer size and intricate Neo-Byzantine and Gothic designs. Architecture buffs will find much to appreciate in Sydney's crowded city skyline. **Sydney Architecture Walks** (Ph: 02 8239 2211) undertake some truly classic architectural adventures, presenting a pleasing pastiche of the city's structures.

1. Opera House 2. Harbour Bridge 3. Sydney Cove, Circular Quay 4. The Rocks 5. Parliament House, The Mint, State Library 6. Walsh Bay and the Piers 7. Anzac Bridge 8. Woolloomooloo 9. Government House

Customs House

Customs House, on Alfred Street at Circular Quay, marks the spot where the British Flag was first raised in 1788. Constructed in 1845, it is now one of Sydney's most historic landmarks. The local Indigenous tribe, the Eora people, are reported to have witnessed the First Fleet's arrival. The Aboriginal flag is now permanently flown from the building. For many years, the building served as the primary trade gateway into Australia. It is now a popular meeting place that affords spectacular views of the area.

Another building that captures the essence of Sydney's history is **The Mint,** which was the site of the colony's first mint and is now the headquarters of the **Historic Houses Trust** (Ph: 02 8239 2288, admission free). Today it is a museum, but it was once the south wing of the old Rum Hospital and so resembles **Parliament House,** which was also part of the historic hospital. It sits alongside the immaculately restored **Hyde Park Barracks,** one of Sydney's most admired heritage buildings, constructed in 1819. Heading south along Macquarie Street, a sedate Georgian exterior hides the busy inner workings of the Parliament House of New South Wales, which is opposite the beautiful St Stephen's Cathedral at the top of Martin Place. It can be admired on tours that run for 90 minutes, except on sitting days (Ph: 02 9230 3444, bookings essential). Beside Parliament House is **Sydney Hospital,** offering tours through the site (Ph: 02 9382 7400), and the **Sydney Eye Hospital,** the oldest hospital in Australia and considered an important part of Macquarie Street history. It is also identified by its landmark frontispiece, the *Il Porcellino* wild boar statue. The legend of *Il Porcellino* promises that he brings good luck when his (by now, well-worn) snout is rubbed.

Left to right: **The Mint; Hyde Park Barracks** are just two of the historical buildings found at Hyde Park's northern end.

City of Contrasts

Although a modern and progressive city, Sydney has not forgotten its colonial past. College Street, Macquarie Street and George Street are all ideal places to witness Sydney's development as a city through its architecture. The Rocks also presents an opportunity to view some of Australia's oldest buildings, now imbued with not only an attractive time-stained appeal but also the relaxing open-air feel of Sydney Harbour's waterfront.

Martin Place is a pedestrian mall in the CBD surrounded by many historical buildings.

Hyde Park Barracks Museum was built in 1819 by architect Francis Greenway.

Strand Arcade Opened in 1892, this was the last arcade built in Victorian Sydney.

Paddy's Markets have been an institution in the Haymarket area for over 150 years.

St Mary's Cathedral was erected gradually from 1821 to 2000 and is designed around the geometric, decorated style of Gothic.

Sydney Town Hall, now the seat of city government, was built on the site of a convict burial ground.

Architectural Treasures

Obsessed as it may be with a headlong rush into modernity and cementing its place on the world stage, the city of Sydney has not forgotten its colonial origins. Quaint and characteristic structures provide Sydneysiders with a rich, nostalgia-filled glimpse into the city's past. From one end of the CBD to the other, a significant number of stately architectural structures line the city's thronging streets.

On **Macquarie** and **College Streets**, bordered by **The Domain** and **Hyde Park**, a significant number of Sydney's oldest buildings can be seen. The impressive, columned exterior of the **Mitchell Library** (Cnr Macquarie St and Shakespeare Pl, open 11 a.m. – 5 p.m. daily) is part of the **State Library of New South Wales** and is definitely worth a look. It houses a significant collection of Australian historical records and the mosaic floor in the lobby is simply magnificent. It resembles the style and structure of the **Art Gallery of New South Wales** (Art Gallery Rd, the Domain, Ph: 02 9225 1744, open daily 10 a.m. – 5 p.m.), which was built in a Classical Revival style and combines modern additions.

Many other historic structures dot the Sydney skyline, including the Art Deco splendour of the **Museum of Contemporary Art (MCA)** and **Customs House** at Circular Quay. Beginning at the western end of Broadway, stroll past the magnificent **Gothic Revival clock tower** to lounge on the manicured lawns of **University** of Sydney's Main Quadrangle. This beautiful and ornate heritage site is open to the surrounding buildings, which have been carved from local sandstone in an elaborate Neo-Gothic style. The idea was to retain the Main Quad's Gothic feel while the Science Road developed its distinctive Mediterranean style. Another impressive clock tower at the eastern end of Broadway marks the location of Sydney's historic **Central Station**, another heritage-listed building built on a site that was once a cemetery, convent, police barracks and morgue. It is now Sydney's main train station for metropolitan and **CountryLink** rail transport.

Queen Victoria's Statue, outside the Queen Victoria Building on Town Hall Place, facing Town Hall.

Further along George Street, the fast pace of Sydney life takes a backseat to quiet reflection in the city's selection of heritage churches and cathedrals, such as **St Andrew's**, consecrated in 1868 and restored to its current state in 2000. It is situated opposite the heritage-listed **Sydney Town Hall** and **QVB** on the corner of George and Park Streets.

Perhaps most overlooked of all Sydney's heritage buildings is the exquisite **Strand Arcade**, declared a heritage site at a time when developers were looking to raze the historic arcade and replace it with a multi-level CBD carpark.

Concealed between the busy thoroughfares of George Street and Pitt Street Mall, the Strand Arcade sits in the shadow of the futuristic **Sydney Tower**.

Pitt Street Mall The heart of the CBD's retail area houses beautiful department stores and the impressive Strand Arcade.

Heritage Buildings

Macquarie Street bears the name of the State's fifth Governor, Lachlan Macquarie. This stretch of road represents one of his major works and the city's first significant construction boom occurred during his tenure. Macquarie commissioned some of Sydney's most noted structures. His vision of Macquarie Street's grand old heritage buildings line the left side of the road as it leads downhill from Hyde Park to the Opera House and Circular Quay. The right side of the road contains the rooms of many of Sydney's leading doctors, Macquarie Street being the preferred address for the city's medical fraternity.

Queen Victoria Building

Occupying an entire city block on George Street between Park and Market Streets, QVB was designed by architect George McRae and completed in 1898, replacing the original Sydney markets.

Its construction occurred during difficult times when Sydney was in recession. The building's grandiose, "Romanesque" design evolved from a calculated decision to help generate employment.

The exterior is dominated by a massive dome-shaped roof, a centrepiece decorated by statues and stained-glass windows that allow natural light to fill the building's multistorey interior. Suspended from the roof's interior is a large Victorian-styled clock that chimes on the hour.

The glass ceilings of the Strand Arcade permit upward views of the modern architecture that now conceals the arcade and makes it one of Sydney's best-kept secrets. Comprised of three levels of unusual and tasteful shops to explore, it will keep many visitors entertained and enthralled for hours. Retail shopping, combined with a dash of history, enhances any visitor's outing.

The **Sydney Opera House** is one of the most recent additions to Sydney's impressive collection of heritage buildings. It received its National Heritage listing in July 2005.

Right: **Parliament House of New South Wales,** in Macquarie Street, was once the northern wing of the old Rum Hospital.

The Rocks

Circular Quay and **The Rocks** represent the true heart of Sydney's colonial days. **George Street North**, running from the underpass underneath **Circular Quay station** at **Alfred Street** and the **Cahill Expressway** to the foundation stones of **Sydney Harbour Bridge** at **Dawes Point**, is Sydney's oldest roadway. Along this stretch of street you can find some of the city's finest tourist attractions and historic structures.

Above, clockwise from left: **Campbells Cove; Argyle St; Cadmans Cottage** Step back in time and enjoy the surrounds of these three extremely important historic attractions at The Rocks.

Approximately 1150 people arrived from Britain aboard the eleven ships of the First Fleet. Of these, two-thirds were convicts. Along with the soldiers sent to guard them, they settled the area of Sydney now known as The Rocks. The convicts constructed public buildings and homes for government officials and settlers and, by the 1820s, Sydney had a road system and police force. These original buildings were made of local sandstone, from which the name The Rocks was derived.

Convict transportation ceased in 1840 and Sydney was officially declared a city, becoming capital of New South Wales in 1842. The State originally occupied the whole eastern half of Australia but was later segmented into Victoria and Queensland. The Rocks now contains the largest concentration of Sydney's heritage buildings.

While there is certainly much for the visitor to see and do along George Street North, much of the appeal of The Rocks can also be traced to its quiet laneways and residential backstreets, and a proper visit to The Rocks should include some time spent in these quaint and less-trafficked areas of Australia's birthplace.

Leading off George Street is **Argyle Street**, leading uphill to the towering **Argyle Cut**. On the way you will pass the heritage-listed **Argyle Stores** (12–20 Argyle Street), a collection of intriguing small businesses selling goods of local appeal.

Campbells Cove

Campbells Cove is an attractive little bay nestled in the shadow of the southern end of Sydney Harbour Bridge. Situated between Dawes Point Park and Circular Quay West, it is the site of the immense Overseas Passenger Terminal near The Rocks district. Campbells Cove is also where the historic HMAS *Bounty* is moored. There is a choice of sunny, ever-popular outdoor eateries on the waterfront.

Argyle Cut has significance as a passageway across The Rocks and adds to the district's character. Originally, a large rock precipice cut The Rocks area in two, creating a major barrier for transportation between The Rocks and Millers Point. Prior to this Argyle Street was in two parts. In 1832, a plan for the Argyle Cut was drawn up and work on it began in 1843 by convict chain gangs. It was the last major Sydney project to use convict labour. However, transportation had ended in 1840 and local residents were rattled by the sight of convict chain gangs, so the Government abandoned the Argyle Cut when it was still only half finished. It was eventually completed by the Sydney Municipal Council using explosives in 1859.

With the building of the **Sydney Harbour Bridge** in the 1920s, the Argyle Cut was widened and the **Bradfield Highway** (leading onto the Harbour Bridge to the north) was completed in 1932.

The highway is a symbol of Sydney's fast-paced, contemporary lifestyle (when compared to its horse-drawn colonial days). As you emerge from the Argyle Cut, a short walk takes you to **Lower Fort Street**, one of The Rocks finest residential thoroughfares.

Things to See and Do

1 Survey Sydney from Observatory Hill.

2 Sample a local ale in one of The Rocks' oldest pubs.

3 Enjoy shopping and people-watching on George Street North.

4 Take a moonlit stroll through The Rocks.

5 Visit the thriving Rocks Market (held on weekends) in the shadow of the Sydney Harbour Bridge on George Street North.

Above, left: **Sydney Observatory** boasts exhibitions of astronomy.
Above, right: **Campbells Cove,** where visitors have a chance to see restored examples of early buildings at Campbells Stores.

Observatory Hill, one of the loveliest parks in Sydney, houses the **Sydney Observatory Museum** (Ph: 02 9217 0481, bookings essential), offering stargazers a chance to delve into astronomy. Towards the **Harbour Bridge** some of The Rocks most popular and historic pubs can be found; these include the **Hero of Waterloo**, a truly old-fashioned Rocks experience, and the **Lord Nelson** on Kent Street. Both are heritage-listed buildings, as is the equally impressive **Palisade Hotel**, a tall, thin tower on a hilltop in Bettington Street. The **Australian Hotel**, another popular and heritage-listed pub, is situated on **Cumberland Street** (running parallel with the Bradfield Highway as it leads onto the Sydney Harbour Bridge). Nearby is **Susannah Place** (58–64 Gloucester Street), a row of four petite, working-class terrace houses and a corner store built in 1844. The store sells retro-styled goods from the era of its original construction.

Of an even older vintage is **Cadmans Cottage** (110 George Street North), built in 1815 and once a barracks originally attached to stores and a dockyard on Sydney Cove. It is Sydney's oldest cottage, named after ex-convict John Cadman who moved into the cottage in 1827. Now it houses a museum and the **Sydney Harbour National Park Information Centre** (Ph: 02 9247 5033). Next door is the **Sydney Visitor Centre**, which provides some interesting and informative insights on Sydney's past (Ph: 1800 067 676).

Nearby on the waterfront is **Campbells Cove**, an attractive little harbour where the HMAS *Bounty* replica is moored in between its tours of the harbour. The cove provides exquisite views of Sydney Opera House and the Harbour Bridge. Campells Stores, an example of 19th-century warehouses now rare in Sydney, provides a nostalgic backdrop to any event. Campbells Stores features the very relaxed and stylish **Waterfront Restaurants**.

Right, top to bottom: **The Sydney Visitor Centre, Rocks Square; The Rocks Market; The Rocks Ghost Tours** Take the time to discover everything on offer at The Rocks; stroll the markets or scare yourself on a Ghost Tour (Ph: 1300 731 971).

Modern Architectural Feats

With an intriguing contrast of old-world buildings and futuristic skyscrapers, Sydney appeals to many kinds of edificial taste. With the addition of modern designs and the sheer presence of its taller structures, Sydney's CBD is graced with the most notable and awe-inspiring skyline in Australia. Whether visitors wish to observe Sydney's grand panorama, or acknowledge the beauty of its towering modern architecture, the city has many great vantage points. Take the time to not only enjoy the historical wonders that still grace the city today, but also to recognise the talents of more recent architectural geniuses.

No trip to Sydney is complete without a visit to **Sydney Tower** (100 Market Street, open 9.30 a.m. – 10.30 p.m. daily). Opened in 1981 and now the city's tallest building, it gives outstanding views of Sydney, the Blue Mountains and the Pacific Ocean. From the tower, visitors will be able to observe a full panorama of city buildings from one position. The **MLC Centre** on Martin Place was Sydney's tallest building from 1977 to 1992 (at 244 m above sea level) and was awarded the Sir John Sulman medal by the Royal Australian Institute of Architects.

Modern City Centre High-rise buildings dominate the skyline; however, many historical treasures are juxtaposed with new architecture and both styles can be equally admired.

Roughly bounded by George Street in the east, Darling Harbour in the west, King Street Wharf to the north and Broadway to the south, the CBD also contains **World Square** (Cnr George and Liverpool Streets), a massive shopping complex on what was once one of Sydney's premier retail outlets, Anthony Hordern and Sons. Before the building of the Sydney Harbour Bridge, the World Square site was the home of retail therapy in Sydney. Demolished in the early 1980s, the site lay dormant for over 20 years until recent work. Today 90 stores, spanning three storeys and an entire city block, are situated within World Square. The **Sydney Monorail** makes a stop here, and the many cafés, restaurants, bars, hotels and supermarket facilities make it the shopping precinct of choice for many city residents.

Left to right: **AXA Building; Sydney Tower; World Square** — just some of the more recent displays of architectural prowess.

Higher Elevations

Left to right: Sydney Tower; Sydney Port's Harbour Control Tower.

Night-owls and after dark revellers can obtain elevated views of the city from the ANA Hotel's spectacular Horizons Bar (176 Cumberland St, The Rocks) and at the Astral Bar on the 17th floor of Star City Casino. Alternatively, the Summit Restaurant provides 360° revolving views from the 47th floor of Australia Square. Other attractive spots include the revolving restaurant of Sydney Tower. At 300 m above sea level, the restaurant also has incredible 360° panoramic views. For yet another perspective, try the 25th floor cocktail bar and restaurant in the long-standing Boulevard Hotel on William Street.

Other recent and notable additions to the Sydney skyline include the **Allianz Centre** (2 Market Street), fronting onto Darling Harbour and Cockle Bay on the western edge of the CBD. Some visitors might recognise this building from its cameo in the blockbuster film *The Matrix*. It provided a gleaming backdrop to the famous "bullet-time" rooftop battle and helicopter crash. The equally impressive **AXA Building**, with its shimmering glass exterior, offers prime views of the harbour and Botanic Gardens from its heavily windowed elevations near Circular Quay. A true marvel to behold, the Sydney Opera House (at Bennelong Point on the eastern side of Circular Quay) remains one of Australia's most recognised and celebrated icons. When Jørn Utzon began designs for the famous structure in 1955, the visionary Danish architect conceived Sydney's finest centre for culture and the arts. Fifty years later, his work of art has become instantly synonymous with Australia.

Not Afraid of Heights?

Today, visitors can take advantage of the height of Sydney's buildings through organised tours. The most recent of these is the **Skywalk** tour of Sydney Tower (Ph: 02 9333 9200). The open-air access to the building's rooftop viewing platform is nothing short of spectacular. Suspended over the edge of the Tower, those game enough to take on the challenge will be rewarded with 360° views at a height of 260 m above sea level. Together with the Sydney Harbour Bridge's **BridgeClimb** (5 Cumberland St, The Rocks, www.bridgeclimb.com, Ph: 02 8274 7777), these are two of the best and most popular tours available for viewing Sydney's glittering expanse.

Bridge Climb Game visitors take on the personal challenge of climbing to the top of the Sydney Harbour Bridge to relish the outstanding city views.

BridgeClimb gives willing thrillseekers the chance to survey the harbour and its surrounds from the peak of Sydney Harbour Bridge. Climbs take place hourly from dusk to dawn. Taking 3½ hours, this includes a thorough briefing and safety demonstration to ensure climbers are fully prepared for a unique and exhilarating experience. Whether old or new, intricately evocative or sparsely minimal, there are many architectural wonders to be seen and experienced in Sydney's CBD.

Left to right: **Allianz; Bert Flugelman's "Pyramid Tower"; HSBC Building** Modern office buildings give the skyline its imposing presence and are often enhanced by cutting-edge sculptures situated nearby in surrounding squares and courtyards.

City Arts and Entertainment

The area stretching from Broadway and Central Station (along George Street up to Hyde Park in the north and Darling Harbour and Pyrmont in the west) is home to some of Sydney's most vibrant and popular nightlife and entertainment locales. Within roughly a square kilometre radius is a plethora of nightspots and cultural centres.

Break a Leg

Darling Harbour's eateries and bars generate non-stop energy and excitement. From the outrageous 24/7 glitz of **Star City Casino** to the lively oriental eateries of **Chinatown**, there is no limit to the number of venues visitors can attend. On sunny days and neon-lit nights, entertainment abounds. The crowded **George Street Cinema Complex** is a hub for movie buffs. Lovers of live performance can catch shows at the **Sydney Entertainment Centre**, the **Lyric Theatre** and the long-standing **Capitol Theatre**.

Around **Martin Place** are several other distinguished Sydney theatres and venues, including the exquisite **State Theatre** (opened in 1928 and the only theatre that still captures the grandeur of Hollywood's heyday), **Theatre Royal** and the **City Recital Hall** (Angel Place, parallel to Martin Place between George and Pitt Street, Ph: 02 8256 2222).

1. Maritime Museum **2.** Harbourside Shopping Centre **3.** South Steyne **4.** Convention Centre **5.** Tumbalong Park **6.** The Outback Centre **7.** IMAX Theatre **8.** Cockle Bay Wharf **9.** Sydney Aquarium

Left to right: **Train at Darling Harbour; Chinese Garden of Friendship; Tumbalong Park** Darling Harbour has much to entertain adults and children alike. Enjoy the gorgeous surrounds of the Chinese Garden of Friendship, the largest garden of its type outside mainland China. Just north of the gardens is Tumbalong Park, a large playground area sure to amuse children. Not far from the playground are paddle boats, bungee trampolines, a mini-train, carousel, theme parks and the IMAX Theatre.

Sydney Aquarium

Children and adults will be enthralled by the Sydney Aquarium, where visitors can walk through a giant perspex tunnel beneath a tank holding 1.5 million litres of water and recreating part of Sydney Harbour. With over 5000 sea creatures and more than 50 specialised displays, visitors can view exhibits of penguins, seals, sharks, crocodiles, Platypuses and magnificent specimens from the Great Barrier Reef (Ph: 02 9262 2300, open daily 9.30 a.m. – 10 p.m.).

Entertainment Arenas

Star City Casino
80 Pyrmont Street, Pyrmont
(Ph: 02 9777 9000)

Ticketek
195 Elizabeth St, Hyde Park
(Ph: 13 2849)

Sydney Entertainment Centre
35 Harbour St, Darling Harbour
(Ph: 13 6100)

Capitol Theatre
13 Campbell St, Haymarket
(Ph: 1300 136 166)

Theatre Royal
MLC Centre, 108 King St, Sydney
(Ph: 02 9224 8444)

Hoyts George Street Cinema
505 George St, Sydney
(Ph: 02 9273 7431)

State Theatre
49 Market St, Sydney
(Ph: 02 9373 6852)

Fun-filled Learning

Entertaining children has never been easier — Sydney city has plenty to keep them amused. **The Outback Centre** (Ph: 02 9283 7477) and **Sydney Wildlife World** (next to Sydney Aquarium, Ph: 02 9333 9288) are two great options. Wildlife World is home to over 6000 animals, including some of Australia's most bizarre native species. Enjoy movies by the waterfront at the **IMAX Theatre,** which has the world's largest cinema screen. Several different films are shown each day from 10 a.m. – 10 p.m. (Ph: 02 9281 3300). Try a spooky alternative on the **History, Convicts and Murders Most Foul Tours** of The Rocks at night (Ph: 02 9555 2700). It is an entertaining and offbeat way to learn about the history of the area.

Festivals to Delight All

Chinatown, Darling Harbour and Star City all come to life each year during Chinese New Year festivities when dragon boat races are held in the marina at Darling Harbour and Star City Casino is decorated in Chinese-themed garb. Theatre lovers will find the area a blessing thanks to the many stage and cinema halls. Arts festivals are another popular institution. The annual **Sydney Writers' Festival** (Ph: 02 9252 7729) brings together local and international authors. The **Sydney Film Festival** runs for two weeks and features independent films from all around the world (Ph: 02 9373 6655). The closure of Victoria Street's roadway on the outskirts of Kings Cross for the Film Festival's awards night is a highlight.

The Art of Shopping

From trendy designer labels to bargain vintage clothing, Sydney city has shopping to satisfy the most eclectic tastes. There are shopping precincts on Pitt, George, Elizabeth and Castlereagh Streets, where visitors will find traditional department stores in large shopping arcades such as the **Imperial, Centrepoint, Skygarden, Piccadilly** and the **Strand Arcade** (www.sydneycity.nsw.gov.au gives help on where to go and what to find). **Paddy's Market** (**Market City Complex**, Haymarket) has been Sydney's bargain shopping outlet for 150 years. Paddy's is the largest market in Australia and even the most particular bargain hunters will find what they seek here.

Top to bottom: **Lyric Theatre at Star City; Sydney Theatre** These theatres are just two in the myriad of complexes that entertain visitors with their range of local and international acts.

Top to bottom: **QVB; Sydney Central; The Strand Arcade** Shopping is made even more enjoyable in these tastefully designed complexes.

25

Eternity Man

In the 1930s, Arthur Stace, a homeless man living in Sydney, wrote the word "Eternity" in every doorway, street and major entrance to a public place or building in Sydney. After his conversion to Christianity, Stace had heard an evangelist say "Eternity! Eternity! Oh, that this word could be emblazoned across the streets of Sydney!" Stace then spent the next 40 years enscribing "Eternity" all over the city in yellow chalk. In 1956, the mysterious scribe's identity was uncovered by Stace's church pastor, who caught Stace in the act, yellow-handed. To pay homage to "the Eternity man", a huge Eternity sign, written in Stace's distinctive handwriting, was illuminated on the Harbour Bridge during the fireworks finale at the opening ceremony of the Sydney Olympic Games in 2000.

The Museum of Contemporary Art displays modern art.

Museum of Sydney shows colonial and contemporary art.

Police Justice Museum has the history of law on display.

City Galleries and Museums

If Sydney's typically sunny climate suddenly turns grey, visitors can always take refuge in one of the city's world-class museums. **Art Gallery Road**, leading through the Domain from St Mary's Cathedral down to the Sydney Harbour foreshores at Mrs Macquaries Point, is the site of the **Art Gallery of New South Wales**, now a massive repository of Australian, European and Asian art, which presents nearly 40 different exhibitions annually. The gallery also houses the **Yiribana Gallery**, the world's largest exhibition of Aboriginal and Torres Strait Islander artwork, which it displays exclusively.

The Art Gallery of New South Wales is an imposing building featuring a classical Greek portico.

In addition to the superb collection of artwork inside the Art Gallery of New South Wales, the building's beautiful sandstone exterior also commands attention. The outside is decorated with impressive bronze bas-relief panels depicting "distinctive historical art periods": Assyrian, Egyptian, Grecian, Roman, Gothic and Renaissance. Although twelve blank panels exist on the gallery's exterior, only four bas-relief works were ever completed, now seen at the southern end of the gallery's entrance.

The **Museum of Contemporary Art (MCA)**, on the waterfront at Circular Quay West, contains a more cutting-edge style of art. Situated in the old Maritime Services Board premises, the MCA opened in 1991 at the site of the First Fleet's mooring in 1788. It is Sydney's most notable contemporary art house and has several very popular venues available for hire, with spectacular views of Sydney Harbour and the Opera House.

Art by the Water

A number of other renowned museums are situated around the foreshore, including Darling Harbour's **Australian National Maritime Museum** (2 Murray St, Darling Harbour, Ph: 02 9298 3777). A 40 m high signal mast, with maritime pennant flags hoisted daily to report on the city's weather conditions, marks the location of the museum's western entrance.

Resting in the shade beneath Pyrmont Bridge and the massive Australian flag tower, the Australian National Maritime Museum's collection documents Australia's waterways and seafaring history.

On the eastern side of the museum, in the harbour's waters, are several of its most visited attractions: a collection of historic vessels that include a racing cutter dating from 1888; HMAS *Vampire*, an ex-RAN destroyer from 1952; *Onslow*, an Oberon-class submarine from 1968; the *John Lewis*, a pearling lugger from Broome; and a "floating lighthouse" (unmanned light-tower) painted in an eye-catching shade of bright red.

Along with the other, mostly operational, historic vessels, the museum's fleet makes a truly superb spectacle against a backdrop of the modern Sydney CBD skyline. These "floating museums" are also complemented by a series of popular temporary exhibitions on display throughout the year. **Sydney Heritage Fleet** (Wharf 7, Pirrama Road, Pyrmont) also documents Sydney's maritime history with its fleet of working historic vessels.

The nearby Broadway and Parramatta Road lead to the **University of Sydney** where Macleay Museum (Ph: 02 9351 2274) began as a repository for the vast collections of **Alexander Macleay**, a noted Briton who was appointed Colonial Secretary of New South Wales under Governor Darling in 1825. Macleay brought his impressive collection with him from England to Sydney. Today, the museum displays a large, eclectic assortment of vertebrate and invertebrate animal collections, historical photographs, ethnography and vintage scientific instruments.

Australian Museum With its frontages to William and College Street, the museum presides over the eastern reaches of Hyde Park. It is the oldest museum in Australia.

Science, History and the Law Explained

Nearby, behind Darling Harbour in the reinvigorated residential area of Ultimo and Pyrmont, sits the **Powerhouse Museum** (500 Harris Street, Ultimo, Ph: 02 9217 0111), a popular treat with kids of all ages and with school groups. The museum, redesigned around the original power station that supplied electricity to Sydney's trams, has an incredible collection of over 385,000 objects.

The collection spans the areas of science, technology, industry and space exploration, amongst others. The Powerhouse houses some 22 permanent exhibitions, plus short-term exhibitions, complemented by its ever-popular interactive displays. Along with the historic **Sydney Observatory** at The Rocks, these museums together constitute the **Museum of Applied Arts and Sciences.**

On the eastern side of Circular Quay sits the **Justice and Police Museum** (Cnr Phillip and Albert Sts, Ph: 02 9252 1144, open 10.00 a.m. – 5.00 p.m.). Made from imposing sandstone slabs and fortified by a gate of iron spikes, the site was a police court during the late 19th century and has been beautifully restored. The Justice and Police Museum houses many macabre and chilling artefacts from its past. These include mug shots of Sydney's most notorious criminals, a number of weapons, as well as recreations of old magistrates courtrooms, police charge rooms and remand cells.

The **Museum of Sydney** (Cnr Bridge and Phillip Sts Circular Quay, Ph: 02 9251 5988, open daily 9.30 a.m. – 5.00 p.m.) is built on the site where, in 1788, Governor Arthur Phillip constructed the first Government House (seat of authority for the first nine Governors of New South Wales). It offers a glimpse into old Sydney life, taking visitors on an evocative journey of discovery through Sydney's pre-colonial days and beyond. The exhibitions and technology bring to life stories of Indigenous culture, environment, commerce, authority, colonisation and the workaday life of Sydneysiders throughout the years. Other relics of the past can be found at the **Australian Museum** (Cnr College and William Sts, opposite Hyde Park, Ph: 02 9320 6000), and the **Sydney Jewish Museum** (148 Darlinghurst Rd, Ph: 02 9360 7999) where permanent and temporary exhibitions focus on the events of the WWII Holocaust and Jewish life in Sydney from the first days of European settlement.

The Australian Museum, established in 1827, is Australia's first museum, and has earned international acclaim in natural history, natural science, cultural artefacts and Indigenous studies research. It also houses several significant temporary exhibitions each year and gives detailed insights into local history with its emphasis on collections from the Pacific region. Close by is the **Reserve Bank of Australia** (65 Martin Place) where you can visit the **Museum of Australian Currency Notes**, opened in 2005. Its stated aims are to display currency notes and related material from bank archives and to tell the story of how Australia's currency notes have reflected the country's economic and political development.

Powerhouse Museum has 11 km worth of exhibitions.

Maritime Museum An important repository of Australian heritage.

Parks and Gardens

Sydney's collection of city parklands represent the city's "green lungs", and are as popular with city office workers relaxing on their lunch breaks as they are with visitors to Sydney. These places provide a welcome respite from the concrete jungle's hectic pace.

Hyde Park, split into two halves by Park Street, is Sydney's urban Arcadia. Each half of this pleasant space contains its own showpiece structure. There is Archibald Fountain in the north, unveiled in 1932 in honour of Australia's contribution to the Great War in France. In the southern half of the park stands the Anzac War Memorial, C. Bruce Dellit's spectacular Deco-classicist creation, which serves as Sydney's main commemorative military monument. Wide boulevards lead pedestrians, flanked by a canopy of 100-year-old Moreton Bay Figs, through the centre of each half of the park.

The Royal Botanic Gardens are a landscaped oasis on the edge of the harbour, offering tranquility and escape from the daily grind.

At the park's southern end is the Museum train station, with St James Station on Elizabeth Street to the north. Both are part of Sydney's "City Circle" CBD train line. On the opposite side of College Street, flanking Hyde Park's eastern edge, is the more modern, concrete and steel Cook and Phillip Park, housing a popular swimming pool, recreation centre and a large tiled courtyard to the north. It is the unofficial home of Sydney's skateboarding community and lies in the shadow of St Mary's Cathedral's massive spires. With open spaces, numerous trees, fountains, terraces, artworks and gardens, the park provides a leisurely environment with the added bonus of sporting facilities.

Archibald Fountain in Hyde Park forms a majestic centrepiece to the park.

Dawes Point Park under the Sydney Harbour Bridge is a lush and serene area overlooking the water.

Behind St Mary's sits the Domain, once the private reserve of Governor Arthur Phillip in 1788. It is now an expressive parkland that frequently hosts major concerts. The **Sydney Festival**, held each January, uses the Domain's lawn to showcase its popular jazz evenings.

Also on the Sydney waterfront is **Dawes Point Park,** situated underneath the Sydney Harbour Bridge's southern pylons. The park provides an elegant and ever-popular venue for weddings.

Most Sydney parks are strictly alcohol-free except when they form a venue for major public events — the hugely popular **Annual Food and Wine Fair** held in Hyde Park each October is one such case.

Hyde Park This tasteful area provides its visitors with a welcome respite from the occasionally unnerving and torrid city pace.

Things to See and Do

1   Enjoy free guided walks through the Royal Botanic Gardens; walks leave the Visitors Centre most days at 10.30 a.m.

2   Catch the trackless train for a scenic tour with informative commentary through the Royal Botanic Gardens.

3   In the Domain, under the trees near the Art Gallery, listen to the soap box speakers who have their say and are willing to discuss or argue their point with bystanders.

4   Take a dip in the Olympic pool at Cook and Phillip Park.

Royal Botanic Gardens

The Royal Botanic Gardens comprises 30 ha of carefully manicured gardens and trees. It includes the National Herbarium of NSW with its Botanical Identification Service, the HongkongBank Oriental Garden, the Sydney Tropic Centre and the Rare and Threatened Plants Garden. When combined, this massive area is considered to be the city centre's most carefully detailed and presented green space. The gardens feature an attractive, gradual slope down the water's edge at Farm Cove, offering delightful views out to Fort Denison and Kirribilli and across the North Sydney skyline. A wide pedestrian promenade follows the cove's sea wall, leading west to the Sydney Opera House and Circular Quay, and east to Mrs Macquaries Point.

Several old watering holes can be found in The Rocks district, giving pub-hopping a colonial twist. Try the Orient Hotel at 87 George Street, constructed from 1843–1844, or the Hero of Waterloo in Lower Fort Street, which has not changed much since last century. Interestingly, The Fortune of War on George Street is believed to have the longest continuous liquor licence in Sydney.

Town Hall, surrounded by the city's glittering symphony, lights up the night sky.

Lord Nelson Hotel is situated on the corner of Kent and Argyle Street, The Rocks.

Harbour Bridge An incredible view from many perspectives.

City at Night

Sydney's status as Australia's global city has been enhanced by its reputation as an outgoing party town. The successful hosting of major events, combined with Sydney's friendly residents, have all added to the city's convivial atmosphere. A variety of locations in the city centre and its immediate surrounds have become noted nightlife areas.

When the Sun Goes Down

Close to the CBD, The Rocks, George Street and the Darling Harbour precinct are popular mainstream venues. On the outskirts of central Sydney, **Oxford Street, Newtown** (with its alternative and student population) and **Kings Cross,** with its flashing lights and bawdy reputation, are wilder and more "out there" destinations.

East Sydney and **Darlinghurst** also have a number of nightlife precincts that make up some of Sydney's busiest and most vibrant "after dark" entertainment areas. The western side of Darling Harbour is where you'll find Harbourside, Darling Harbour's massive shopping complex, and the thriving **Star City Casino** complex, which keeps punters and party-goers entertained 24/7. The eastern shores of Darling Harbour also cater to clubbers in the form of **Home**, one of the Southern Hemisphere's largest nightclubs.

Top to bottom: **Chinatown; Kings Cross** These lively environs typify the energy and sensory experience that is Sydney by night.

Cold Beer, Anyone?

The Rocks is also popular for its lively pubs and for its endurance-testing "pub crawls". Situated on **Cowper Wharf Road**, this dock-like area of inner Sydney also has some noted and long-standing pubs, such as the **Woolloomooloo Bay Hotel** and the **Bells Hotel**. The dockside suburb of **Woolloomooloo**, resting between Kings Cross and the Domain parkland in the city, is also a popular spot thanks to a revamped **Finger Wharf**, the chic "W" hotel and its popular local pubs.

Closer to William Street, on the multi-lane freeway leading between the city and Kings Cross, the **Boulevard Hotel** has a 25th-floor cocktail bar with panoramic views and tasteful decor while, a little closer to street level, the **East Sydney**, on **Crown Street**, retains a classic and beautifully retro 1900s pub feel.

The Opera House and Sydney Harbour Bridge, aglow at night, looks magical.

Darling Harbour On many occasions throughout the year, fireworks exploding over the harbour make a night in Sydney extremely memorable.

Cockle Bay Wharf features restaurants with waterfront views.

Dining Out

The **Three Wise Monkeys Pub, Century Tavern, City of Sydney RSL, Cheers Bar** and **Sydney's Spanish Quarter** all centre around the busy intersection of **George** and **Liverpool Streets** next to the massive **World Square** high-rise development. They are perhaps the best spots for wining and dining in this great central location.

As you head further west along Liverpool Street you reach Darling Harbour and **Cockle Bay Wharf**. Along with **King Street Wharf** at the far northern end of Cockle Bay Wharf, this area is recognised for its bars and restaurants with a noticeably alfresco waterfront feel. On busy **Crown Street** is **Sydney's Hard Rock Café**, complete with its rock music memorabilia and international clientele.

Chinatown has a superb selection of eateries, pubs and clubs varying from lavish restaurants to quick, cheap meals in their food halls. Glebe's **Glebe Point Road** has a relaxed and funky feel thanks to its wide selection of restaurants and cafés. While lunchtime in Hyde Park is a common ritual for many of Sydney's office workers, visitors should explore the range of delightful eateries on offer in central Sydney. The **Strand Arcade** houses several classy vintage coffee shops. East Sydney's **Little Italy** (Norton Street, Leichhardt) is the place to find fresh fruit and vegetables or imported Italian foods. Leichhardt is also home to a vibrant Italian population, and the Italian Forum, a residential and commercial complex, bustles with restaurants, cafés, and food retailers.

The **Sydney Fish Market,** on the far side of Darling Harbour and Ultimo, has a pleasant waterfront location and lots of tasty, well-priced treats. Closer to town, the recently developed **Liverpool Lane** (World Square, near George Street and Chinatown) has some enticing oriental eateries, several hotels and some lively pubs.

Sydney's inner suburbs share The Rocks' colonial feel and provide some of Sydney's best café culture. The relaxed, informal feel of these stylish areas is a pleasant respite from Sydney's otherwise frenetic city centre.

No matter what time of night, there is always somewhere in the city to eat, drink and be entertained. Taking in the sight of the Opera House and the Sydney Harbour Bridge twinkling with lights is a great way to cap off an evening's revelry and a sure way to make any night out feel complete.

Star City Casino

Star City Casino, at the northwestern end of Darling Harbour, is entertainment writ large. It offers a complete range of gaming tables, slot machines and other games of chance to serious gamblers and its huge clientele of casual punters.

The venue has a mass of entertainment facilities, including a beautiful 17th-floor cocktail lounge with sweeping, high-rise views of Sydney Harbour, more than 20 restaurants and bars and two theatres that feature a range of acts including live music, comedies, dramas and dancing.

The Star City complex also boasts a five-star hotel, a business centre, banquet and conference rooms, a health club, and a range of retail outlets.

Sydney Suburbs

Variegated Fairy-wren

Thanks to a special and truly spectacular coastal location, a significant proportion of Sydney's residential suburbs are close to the water's edge. This includes a majority of eastern, northern and southern Sydney suburbs, which all have distinctive characteristics and plenty of activities to keep any visitor amused.

Sydney's eastern beachside suburbs are chic and popular, being some of Australia's most loved, recognised and visited stretches of shoreline. **Bondi** and nearby **Bronte Beach** are perhaps the most famous, but there is also the very glamorous **Tamarama Beach** (situated between Bondi and Bronte) or the upmarket atmosphere and peaceful waters around **Rose Bay** and **Watsons Bay** to choose from. Some of the shopping in these areas can also be decidedly classy, especially in the slick and heavily retail-oriented suburb of **Double Bay**.

The city's northern beaches, by comparison, are a little more secluded — imbued with a much more traditional Aussie "surf club" and board-riding culture. Despite the seclusion, a visit to the northern suburbs of Sydney — especially the beachside suburbs — is truly worthwhile. It is possible to access many of these suburbs via public transport and, while there is no train service in operation along the northern beaches, a ferry ride across Sydney Harbour (from Circular Quay) brings visitors to **Manly Beach**, noted for its long stretches of sand and its tree-lined boulevard fronting the beach. From here, the northern beaches stretch upward along the coast as Sydney gives way to the vast waterways and national parks beyond **Palm Beach**.

Many consider the visit to Manly to be something of a mandatory journey while holidaying in Sydney — the ferry ride takes in some of Sydney's best tourist icons along the way, including close-up views of **Sydney Harbour Bridge**, the **Opera House**, **Kirribilli House** (the Prime Minister's Sydney residence), **Taronga Zoo**, **North Head** and **Mrs Macquaries Point**.

To the south are the workaday suburbs of **Sutherland Shire**. Its most famous beach, **Cronulla**, is Sydney's only beach beside a train line, thus making it a popular treat for locals and Sydneysiders from further afield.

Even in the western suburbs, the working-class heartland of Sydney, a variety of very attractive suburbs are found on the waterfront of the **Parramatta River** as it heads inland from Sydney Harbour past **Homebush Bay** (site of **Olympic Park**, the venue for the 2000 Olympic Games and many other major sporting events).

Closer to town, some of Sydney's oldest suburbs — vibrant inner-city regions such as **Surry Hills, Glebe, Balmain, Chippendale, Erskineville, Darlinghurst** and **Paddington** — are modern success stories, having become popular (and pricey) residential areas for city workers who appreciate their close proximity to the CBD and re-invented, stylish living. As the Sydney suburbs have expanded outwards, places like Glebe have become increasingly popular thanks to their convenient locations and affordable prices (when compared to the rest of the inner-city and CBD).

Top to bottom: **Bondi Beach; El Alamein Fountain, Kings Cross; Taronga Zoo; Governor's Bathhouse, Parramatta Park.**

Paddington Terraces Beautiful Victorian terrace houses, which once were slums for much of the post-WWII period, are now highly sought-after commodities.

Top to bottom: *Spirit of Tasmania*; Out on the water.

By the Harbour

Although Sydney's suburban heartland is a sprawling inland region stretching to the foothills of the **Blue Mountains**, central Sydney's most visited tourism areas are rarely far from the waterfront. Even the modern Olympic success story and redevelopment of **Homebush Bay** — and there have been many other major events since the Olypmics — is close to the **Parramatta River**.

Darling Harbour contains numerous bars and eateries. The **Sydney Fish Market,** in nearby **Pyrmont**, also serves up many tasty treats for the hungry traveller. It is easily accessed by walking west from **Pyrmont Bridge** at Darling Harbour to **Harris Street**, where the market can be found in the shadow of the eastern end of **Anzac Bridge**.

Heading out on the Water

A ferry service from **Circular Quay** connects The Rocks with Darling Harbour and a number of private tour operators conduct waterside tours of Sydney Harbour and its many attractions.

Looking from Sydney city to the north-east **1.** Kings Cross and Elizabeth Bay **2.** Rushcutters Bay **3.** Darling Point **4.** Double Bay **5.** Point Piper **6.** Rose Bay **7.** Vaucluse and Nielsen Park **8**. Clark Island **9.** Watsons Bay **10.** South Head

Vaucluse

Despite the majestic residences that line the streets and take advantage of the stellar views, much of Vaucluse is parkland, so enjoy a walk around this area, which includes Nielsen Park.

Walking the harbour Hermit Point Foreshore Walk, Vaucluse.

Captain Cook Cruises (Ph: 1800 804 843), **Matilda Cruises** (Ph: 02 9264 7377) and **John Cadman Cruises** (Ph: 02 9206 6666) are some of the bigger players in this market. For more personalised tours you can hire a water taxi and make your own plans. **Harbour Jet Boats** promise a more spectacular journey, offering swift jet boat rides past the harbour's many features. As you pass under the Sydney Harbour Bridge from Circular Quay on the way to Darling Harbour, the ferry service passes **Dawes Point** and **Millers Point** — site of the huge container terminal used for shipping in and out of Sydney Harbour. **Goat Island** can also be seen, due west, when passing under the Harbour Bridge. Aboriginal people call it *Mel-Mel*, which means "the eye". It was named Goat Island because it served as a kind of free-range goat farm for early colonists. Convicts cut sandstone from the island for building purposes in 1833 and tours are held most days (leaving from **Cadmans Cottage**).

The fashionable harbourside suburb of **Balmain** lies ashore of the island where the harbour's waters turn into **Parramatta River** heading upstream. On the northern sides of the harbour's waters, as you pass under the shadow of the Harbour Bridge's wide span, **Kirribilli**, **Blues Point** and **Lavender Bay** can be seen.

South Head and Middle Harbour

South Head, at the tip of **Lady Bay**, was once a fishing community and retains its quaint village feel with old fishermen's cottages still found along the streets. Spectacular ocean views are just a two-minute walk away through grassy **Robertson Park**, across **Gap Road** to **The Gap**. A walking track leads to South Head through a part of **Sydney Harbour National Park**. Another place to visit by the water is **Middle Harbour**, the largest inlet off Port Jackson. Its two sides join across the narrowest point at **The Spit**. Crossing The Spit Bridge, you can walk all the way to **Manly Beach** along the 10 km **Manly Scenic Walkway**, while a bus runs from Spit Road to Manly Wharf, taking in a scenic route uphill overlooking The Spit marina. The bushland covering the area gives **Balmoral Beach**, on **Hunters Bay**, a peaceful and secluded feel, making it popular with families. **Hunters Park** has a bandstand, which is still used for Sunday jazz concerts.

Bridging the Gaps

Back on the southern shores of the **Harbour Bridge, Johnstons Bay, Blackwattle Bay** and **White Bay** lie in the area behind Darling Harbour. The waters of Johnstons Bay meet Blackwattle Bay at **Anzac Bridge**, originally known as the **Glebe Island Bridge**, completed in 1996 and, at 345 m, the longest cable-stayed bridge in the county. As the Parramatta River winds its way further inland it passes **Birkenhead Point** where the wide sweep of **Iron Cove** and the **Iron Cove Bridge**, leading off the main river, can be seen heading south-west.

Top and bottom: For those who can't resist the allure of Sydney's seemingly endless sunshine, the harbour provides the perfect place to enjoy outdoor exploits. Jet skiing, canoeing, cruising on a yacht or just sitting by the water's edge soaking up solar rays are all ideal ways to enjoy Sydney Harbour.

Looking from Seaforth to North Head in a south-easterly direction 1. Seaforth **2.** Spit Bridge **3.** Middle Harbour **4.** Balmoral **5.** Grotto Point **6.** Middle Head **7.** Clontarf **8.** Manly **9.** North Head

North Head

Facing South Head across the opening of the harbour is North Head. This is one of the most scenic areas in Sydney. With its sheer cliffs, harbour views, amazing coastline, and extensive areas of bushland, it is sure to impress. It is a very popular place for picnics and presents amazing sunset views of the city skyline. There are numerous parking bays for lookouts.

Harbour Beaches: Clifton Gardens

There are numerous secluded coves, scenic bays and sheltered beaches around Sydney Harbour. One of the most popular is Clifton Gardens (*right*) in Chowder Bay, Mosman. Fringed by national park, this pretty beach provides a safe retreat from the bustle of the inner suburbs, with public bathing baths, a wharf, a great walking track that passes through the reserve at Chowder Head, and plenty of public facilities.

Double Bay, where visitors can indulge themselves in exclusive shopping. There are many designer label boutiques, art galleries and antique shops.

Beautiful Bays

As **Park Street** heads out of the city centre from **Sydney's Town Hall**, it passes **Hyde Park** and becomes the wide sweep of **William Street**, leading through East Sydney towards the famous Coca Cola sign above Kings Cross. Over the brow of the hill lies **New South Head Road**, the attractive parklands and marina of **Rushcutters Bay** and the upmarket **Cruising Yacht Club of Australia**.

Yarranabbe Park, at the northern end of the marina and bay, is a nice spot for northerly views of the harbour and of the city skyline crowning Elizabeth Bay and Kings Cross to the west. **Rushcutters Bay Park** is equally pleasant and follows the smooth curve of the cove, adorned by a fleet of glistening yachts moored at the water's edge.

Further east along **New South Head Road** lies **Edgecliff**, the area's main business district, and **Double Bay**, a ritzy and expensive area devoted to boutique shopping, five-star hotels and local café society. Double Bay and its residents' penchant for the expensive and exclusive has earned this affluent area the derisive nickname of "Double Pay", a cheeky reference to its "Rodeo Drive" style of sophistication, glamour and hype. Despite this, few can resist the opportunity to wander through its attractive streets and stores.

Double Bay is easily reached from Sydney's city centre via the eastern suburbs train service, with the nearest stop to Double Bay being **Edgecliff Station**.

Camp Cove, Watsons Bay A popular family beach where visitors can start a 1.5 km walk passing Lady Bay to the promontory of South Head.

Left to right: **Vaucluse Bay; Vaucluse House** Vaucluse is arguably Sydney's most exclusive address. At its heart is Vaucluse House, now a museum open to the public. This historic Sydney building was constructed in 1803. In 1827 it became the home of explorer William Wentworth. Along with Blaxland and Lawson, Wentworth made the first successful European crossing of Sydney's Blue Mountains.

Doyles Restaurant, Watsons Bay was Australia's first seafood restaurant, opened in 1885. For five generations since, it has been family-owned and operated.

Macquarie Lighthouse is Australia's first and longest operating navigational lighthouse. Mariners have enjoyed navigational aid at this site since 1791.

Things to See and Do

1. Take the scenic 5 km Coastal Cliff Walk from Christison Park to South Head, taking in the lighthouses and the 80 m cliffs of The Gap, marking the boundary of part of the Sydney Harbour National Park. This and other walks are offered by the Woollahra Council, who also supply a map and pamphlet full of information to help you make the most of your stay in this picturesque area (Ph: 02 9391 7000).

2. Enjoy fish and chips with seaside views at Doyle's Restaurant.

The main drag, New South Head Road, leads to the sumptuous shoreline homes of **Point Piper** — one of Sydney's priciest residential areas. It then leads through popular **Rose Bay**, past the **Royal Sydney Golf Club** into **Vaucluse** and **Watsons Bay**.

Lovely Lighthouses

Hornby Lighthouse, on the headland of **South Head** and **Hornby**, was constructed following two notorious shipwrecks in 1857 and was opened in 1858. During WWII, the lighthouse and its keepers' cottages came under the control of the Australian Army until 1977 when New South Wales Parks and Wildlife took control of the site. South of Watsons Bay and Vaucluse stands **Macquarie Lighthouse**, the first lighthouse in Australia (Ph: 02 8969 213, bookings essential). It was constructed under the command of Governor Macquarie. Francis Greenway, a knowledgeable convict architect, took on the job. Macquaire was so pleased with the quality of Greenway's work that he granted him emancipation for his efforts.

Hornby Lighthouse is painted in eye-catching red and white vertical stripes.

North Head

South Head

Natural History — The Heads

The heads are a collection of coastal bushland and heath environments protected by areas of national park and containing animals that are well suited to these pockets of urban wild. The rugged and sheer sandstone walls of North and South Head sustain low-lying heathland. Sea birds such as cormorants, Rock Warblers and White-bellied Sea Eagles nest on the cliff ledges here. A colony of Long-nosed Bandicoots, one of the few remaining in Sydney, live on North Head, which is also home to a number of reptiles and amphibians, including the rare Red-crowned Toadlet. The woodlands of Dobroyd and Bradleys Head contain Bloodwood forests that are inhabited by possums and bats. Marine life also thrives around the heads, which are great spots for viewing migrating Humpback Whales.

Left to right: Flannel Flower; White-bellied Sea Eagle; Humpback Whale; Firebrick Sea Star.

Seaside Splendour

Sydney Harbour is one of the world's most beautiful natural harbours. Its deep blue waters lap at a series of pretty coves and beach-fringed suburbs. Even the traditionally working-class western suburbs enjoy waterfront locales thanks to the **Parramatta River**, heading inland from Sydney Harbour Bridge.

The harbour is dotted with several noted islands and popular seaside suburbs that benefit from their beautiful harbourside location. **Woolloomooloo Bay** is a fine example — a recently renewed area housing a selection of bars and restaurants beside the bay's modern marina. Surveying the harbour's waters from here or from the nearby **Mrs Macquaries Point**, you can see **Pinchgut (Fort Denison)**, **Shark** and **Clark Islands** to the east out towards the heads.

Activities in the Marine Park

Inland, beyond the wide span of Sydney Harbour Bridge, **Goat Island** is a popular venue for private parties throughout the year, with its spectacular views of the entire harbour. **The National Parks and Wildlife Service** offers a range of organised guided tours of harbour highlights, including an eerie night tour of the ghostly, disused **Quarantine Station** (Ph: 02 9247 5033).

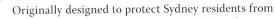
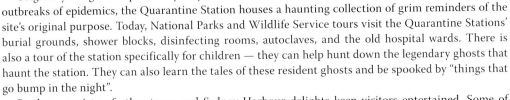

Top to bottom: **Enjoying the waters of Sydney Harbour; Taking in views of the national park at North Head.**

Originally designed to protect Sydney residents from outbreaks of epidemics, the Quarantine Station houses a haunting collection of grim reminders of the site's original purpose. Today, National Parks and Wildlife Service tours visit the Quarantine Stations' burial grounds, shower blocks, disinfecting rooms, autoclaves, and the old hospital wards. There is also a tour of the station specifically for children — they can help hunt down the legendary ghosts that haunt the station. They can also learn the tales of these resident ghosts and be spooked by "things that go bump in the night".

By day, a variety of other tours and Sydney Harbour delights keep visitors entertained. Some of these include the **Fort Denison Brunch**, which is a civilised way to start the day at a site with a rather unsavoury past. Visitors can watch Sydney rouse itself from overnight slumber while enjoying brunch on the fort. The **Middle Head Forts Tour** is also available. With a large number of forts around Sydney, people can explore tunnels, sandstone gun pits and "tiger cages" — purpose-built rooms used to train soldiers in the techniques needed for enduring torture.

Clark Island was named after Lieutenant Ralph Clark, a member of the Sydney Cove Marines who started growing vegetables on the island in 1789.

Killarney Heights is a Middle Harbour suburb that incorporates parts of Garigal National Park.

Fort Denison Just one of several Sydney bastions that are open to the public for tours.

Bradleys Head, where visitors can gain a brilliant view of Sydney Tower and the CBD skyline.

Natural History — Sydney Harbour

Throughout Australia's history, Sydney Harbour has played a crucial role in nurturing many kinds of life. Whether aquatic or terrestrial, endemic or migratory, the harbour is a rich natural habitat and one that is in a constant state of urban flux. Some of its inhabitants (like the Common Ringtail Possum) have adjusted well to city life, co-existing comfortably with humans. Others, like Manly's small colony of Little Penguins, are in a more delicate position, increasingly threatened by the city's growth.

The protected areas within Sydney Harbour National Park — scattered pockets of foreshore bushland and a few small islands — are home to mammals like the Long-nosed Bandicoot, Common Brushtail Possum, Short-beaked Echidna, and Grey-headed Flying Fox. Around 150 species of bird can be observed around Sydney Harbour. Parrots and cockatoos are common in the wooded areas, as are petrels, gulls and egrets around the waterways.

Marine life is also plentiful. Common Dolphins form resident pods in sheltered bays and Southern Right Whales can be seen from coastal headlands. Even Leopard Seals have been found swimming in the harbour.

Bradleys Head is one of the many protected areas around Sydney Harbour.

Left to right: Common Ringtail Possums find sanctuary in the park; An Australian King-Parrot.

The National Parks and Wildlife Service also operates a **Shark Island Ferry Service** every Saturday and Sunday. With a fantastic setting in Sydney Harbour National Park, **Shark Island** is the perfect destination for a weekend picnic. Situated off Rose Bay, it was formerly an animal quarantine area but is popular now for family gatherings. Other ways to access the island are via private boat, **Water Taxis Combined** (Ph: 02 9555 8888), **Taxis Afloat** (Ph: 02 9955 3222) or **Rosman Ferries** (Ph: 02 9955 3458).

Self-guided tours are also a pleasant option. Begin by visiting one of the known points for classic harbour views and just follow your fancy.

Dawes Point Battery Park (under Sydney Harbour Bridge's southern pylons), **Blues Point Reserve** (on the north shore), and the northern promenade of Sydney Opera House present perhaps the most unique viewing opportunities, as does the pedestrian footpath across the Harbour Bridge. **Nielsen Park** in Sydney's east is also another attractive point, popular for picnics and shoreline strolls.

Visit the **Sydney Harbour National Park Information Centre** in **Cadmans Cottage** at The Rocks (110 George Street, The Rocks, Ph: 02 9247 5033) for information and bookings regarding tours to Sydney Harbour's islands and foreshore areas such as **Fort Denison**, the **Quarantine Station**, **Middle Head** and **Bradleys Head**. The centre also provides information on parks and reserves to the west of the city.

Shark Beach, Nielsen Park Beautiful Shark Beach boasts a much-loved stretch of glistening sand, as well as nearby picnic shelters, a gazebo, a large grassed area and a wading beach.

Fox Studios

Fox Studios (Lang Road, Moore Park, Ph: 02 9383 4333) is situated within the old Sydney Showground site, once the venue for the popular Sydney Royal Easter Show (now hosted at Homebush Bay's Olympic Park). The area was leased for 40 years in the late 1990s by a partnership of Rupert Murdoch's News Corporation and Lend Lease for use by Fox Studios. The Fox Studios site was to be used for film, television and video purposes; however, there was no requirement that any area within the site would be used exclusively for this and the Showring is now a vast village green. Most of the site now boasts entertainment, shopping and restaurant facilities. There is also a massive cinema complex and a weekly market every Saturday and Sunday.

Top to bottom: **Bent St, Fox Studios; Bells Hotel, Woolloomooloo.**

Peppermint Lounge, Kings Cross is considered to be one of Sydney's premier lounge bars (situated on Victoria Street, Potts Point).

Eastern Suburbs

Two main thoroughfares lead out of the CBD into Sydney's sunny eastern suburbs: **William Street** (passing through Kings Cross and the exclusive shoreline suburbs) and **Oxford Street,** heading through the hip **Darlinghurst** and **Paddington** districts.

Past Paddington lies the massive urban pastures of **Centennial Parklands** and then **Bondi Junction.** Here **Bondi Road** makes a beeline for the wide stretches of sand at famous **Bondi Beach.**

The area of Sydney between **Oxford Street** and the harbour waters at **Woolloomooloo** contains some of Australia's most colourful living. Wildlife of a different kind inhabits this area and its eccentric, albeit extremely popular, appeal has made **Darlinghurst** Australia's most heavily populated suburb.

Something of a kid-free zone, **Darlinghurst, Potts Point** and **Kings Cross,** together with **Elizabeth Bay,** are characterised by apartment living. Backyards, when found, are generally small in this high-density area. For getting around, try the blue **Bondi and Bay Explorer Bus** which will get visitors to the beaches and through the eastern and south-eastern suburbs including **Double Bay, Bondi, Bronte** and **Coogee.**

Harry's Café de Wheels

The celebrated Harry's Café de Wheels (Cowper Wharf Road, Woolloomooloo) is a caravan-style take-out eatery on the shoreline at Woolloomooloo Bay. A favoured food spot for Sydney cabbies and late-night revellers, this long-standing take-out is noted for its hearty gourmet pies and hot dogs, and includes a variety of largely unique Harry specials. The caravan is permanently parked beside Finger Wharf.

History of Kings Cross

Originally named Queens Cross, the intersection of **William Street** and Darlinghurst was re-named Kings Cross in the early 20th century after England's King Edward VII. During the early to mid 1900s, it was the bohemian heartland of Sydney and a popular residential area for artists, many of whom congregated around the area's coffee shops.

To this day some very popular and long-standing coffee shops continue to service Kings Cross and its surrounds, including the ever-crowded cafés of **Roslyn** and **Victoria Streets** and **Stanley Street** in **East Sydney.**

During the 1960s, Kings Cross became known as a tourism icon and entertainment district. A noted landmark, and favourite meeting place for many, is the **El Alamein Fountain** in Fitzroy Gardens. It was designed by Robert Woodward and erected in 1961 as a memorial to the Ninth Division who fought in the 1942 Battle of El Alamein during WWII.

Kings Cross from above After some years of neglect, the streets and houses surrounding Kings Cross have undergone a revival. Take a stroll along Kellett Street with its striking, late 19th-century terrace houses. Other examples of these refurbished terrace houses are along Victoria Street, which now houses numerous restaurants, bars and cafés.

Left to right: **Oxford Street; Paddington Town Hall; Durty Nelly's Bar, Glenmore Road, Paddington** are some examples of the restored buildings that make this area one of the most beautiful suburbs in Sydney.

Around Kings Cross

Apart from the main drag of Kings Cross (Darlinghurst Road), many of the surrounding streets in this suburb exude a charm that is naturally captivating. **Bayswater Road** is home to some very popular nightclubs and eateries positioned within large, multi-storey terrace houses. **Potts Point** is a spectacular suburb of Art Deco apartment blocks and stylish restaurants, particularly along **Macleay Street.** Despite its close proximity to the flashing lights of Kings Cross, Potts Point manages to retain its distinctive 1920s-era glitz. **Victoria Street** is the heart of the area's café culture. Divided in two by the Kings Cross tunnel leading towards Rushcutters Bay and the eastern suburbs, the southern half of Victoria Street is where the cappuccino and latte flows endlessly, much to the appreciation of the caffeine-loving regulars on this hip stretch of street. The northern half of Victoria Street is an attractive and tree-lined roadway that contains several relaxing restaurants and backpacker hostels as the road leads down to Potts Point.

Classic accommodation can also be found in **Paddington**, where lovingly restored terrace houses complement the chic shopping of **Oxford Street** and the quaint side-streets of this much-visited area. **Woollahra's** leafy locale is distinctly English in manner, as is the stylish melting pot of cafés and bars encircling the Paddington intersection at **Five Ways.** The scarcity of backyards in the inner east's densely populated districts are compensated for by the wide spaces of **Centennial Parklands** and **Moore Park,** the latter also being the site of Sydney's most central golf course. The Centennial of Federation, in 2001, was marked by a massive street parade, resplendent with floats and marching bands, held along the nearby Oxford Street and its adjoining roads. In 1888 Centennial Park was dedicated by Australia's "Father of Federation", Sir Henry Parkes, and was the site for the inauguration of Federation in 1901.

Paddington Markets The markets have a fantastic mix of fashion, jewellery, artworks and collectibles all in one of Sydney's trendiest suburbs. They are open every Saturday and guarantee a day of fun-filled shopping.

Elizabeth Bay House, Potts Point This building, designed by architect John Verge, is a prime example of colonial architecture. The house comprises many tasteful rooms elegantly furnished from the period 1839–1845.

Centennial Park Many activities can be enjoyed in Centennial Park, including horse riding, cycling, ranger-guided tours and picnicking. The park also houses the outdoor Moonlight Cinema on summer nights from December to February. Centennial Parklands comprises three large reserves: Centennial Park, Moore Park and Queens Park. Less than 5 km from the Sydney CBD, Centennial Park is a cherished space for the many residents of the high-density suburbs surrounding it. The park is noted for its attractive lakes.

Bountiful Bondi

A sun-drenched Aussie icon, famous **Bondi Beach** is Australia's most beloved stretch of shoreline. The beach's wide promenade makes for cool, relaxing walks on Sydney's sultry summer afternoons. On warm summer days — and even during other seasons (weather permitting) — the 380 bus service from the city centre to Bondi Beach is invariably crowded. The beach is served by **Campbell Parade**, a broad boulevard running the length of the Bondi shore. To the north of the beach sits the residential area of **Dover Heights** and the attractive **Bondi Golf and Diggers Club** (Ph: 02 9130 3170). The celebrated **Bondi Icebergs Club** (Ph: 02 9130 4804) is found at the southern end of the beach's wide sweep, and beyond this, the **Bondi to Coogee Coastal Walk** follows the curves of the coast as it heads south, taking in chic **Tamarama Beach** and the park-like **Bronte Beach** along the way.

Bondi Festivities

Although always crowded, Bondi's size swells noticeably during some of the annual events held on the beach each year.

Top to bottom: **Bondi Beach art; Bondi Beach from the south** If you are a cyclist, surfer or artist, Bondi has much to keep you entertained. Even quiet contemplation, while looking out over the waves, is a delight.

Aerial view of Bondi Beach from the north Bondi Beach is approximately 1 km long. The width of the beach averages 50 m at the north end, widening out to 100 m at the south end. It is the widest beach in the Sydney region.

Left to right: **MacKenzies Point; Ben Buckler Pool** Waves crash against the shore at these particular points. Visitors can walk over MacKenzies Point and stroll down to Tamarama and Bronte from Bondi. Ben Buckler is just out on the opposite point from MacKenzies Point, a little closer to Bondi Beach.

A camera is an absolute must at the colourful **Bondi Kite Festival**, the **Festival of the Winds**, held each September. It sees the skies above Bondi filled with graceful shapes and colours, as skilled local and international kite handlers and creators display their wares to an enthralled sea of onlookers.

The temperatures heat up dramatically during the action of the annual **City to Surf Race**, which finishes at Bondi Beach. This fun-run attracts tens of thousands of participants each year, from elite athletes to sunburnt, sore and sorry types who limp past the finish line hours after commencing the run on William Street in the city centre. Acknowledged as Australia's premier road run, the City to Surf Race had humble beginnings in 1971, being based on San Francisco's Bay to Breakers marathon. It is generally recognised as the world's largest timed fun-run and, as such, now attracts high-profile international competitors.

Swimming and surfing are the most popular activities on the beach, despite a couple of noted rips including the "Backpacker Express" and "Bronte Express" — the latter said to deliver distraught swimmers direct to Bronte, two beaches south of Bondi. With its population of surfers being complemented by the presence of Jewish and Italian communities, Bondi has a fascinating cultural mix and ambience.

Bondi Heritage

Bondi has some intriguing Aboriginal sites towards the northern end of the beach's headland. At MacKenzies Point, Ben Buckler and around the golf course there are Indigenous rock engravings. All of the engravings have been re-grooved by the Waverley Municipal Council to ensure their continued preservation.

In fact, the word *Bondi* is derived from an Aboriginal word meaning "sound of water breaking on the beach".

Bondi Junction

Bondi Junction is situated roughly a mile uphill from Bondi Beach. "The Junction" is a vibrant and hectic transport hub for the eastern suburbs, containing a train and bus terminus, and Bondi Junction Overpass, the flyover connecting traffic from the Bondi Junction outskirts with Centennial Park and Woollahra.

Bondi Junction has always had a strong emphasis on retailing and it houses one of Sydney's largest shopping precincts. Its major outlets straddle Oxford Street and are linked together by walkways over the Oxford Street traffic. The Oxford Street Mall is the pulsating heartbeat of Bondi Junction retail. An extremely modern and spacious design, it houses numerous big-name homewares and fashion retailers together with several supermarkets and a cinema. Many attractive outdoor cafés can also be found under the canopy of tarpaulins decorating the mall between Bronte Road and Newland Street. The mall is also home to a weekly Organic Food and Farmer's Market, and hosts a weekly Rotary Market every Sunday.

The Jewish community's customs are reflected in Bondi's collection of synagogues and kosher butcher shops. The long-standing **Hakoah Club** (61–67 Hall Street, Ph: 02 9130 3344), one of the Sydney Jewish Community's most important establishments, is not far from the beachfront.

Whatever activities you enjoy on Australia's most loved beach, the experience is always memorable. Christmas day on Bondi has become a tourist tradition as the beach becomes invaded by the bulk of Sydney's backpacker community for festive season celebrations.

Sunday School

A very popular market, which is hosted every Sunday, is in the grounds of Bondi Public School. They have clothing, arts and crafts, bric-a-brac and other collectibles.

Left to right: **Bondi Markets**, just one of the many places visitors can enjoy while in Bondi; **Campbell Parade** is the main street in Bondi. It has plenty of tempting cafés and restaurants to ensure visitors are nourished and content.

The Royal Hotel (2 Perouse Road, Randwick, Ph: 02 9399 3006) dates from 1887 and is a grand and beautiful National Trust building, situated on a prominent street corner. It sits across a small park from the Prince of Wales Hospital, a major teaching hospital that services all of New South Wales. It was originally built in the 1870s using funds made available by public donations.

Top to bottom: **Bondi to Coogee Walk; Clovelly; Gordons Bay to Coogee Walk; Surf lifesaving boats at the ready.**

Glamourous Tamarama and Beyond

Following the coastal walk south from Bondi Beach brings you to the little cove-like beach of **Tamarama,** a glamorous strip of coast favoured by the "beautiful people" of Sydney's eastern suburbs. Beyond this lies **Bronte Beach, Clovelly,** the snorkellers' haven of **Gordons Bay** and **Coogee Beach** (the latter being a popular haunt for British backpackers).

Coogee

Despite gaining its name from an Aboriginal word meaning "bad smell", probably due to seaweed washed up on the beach, Coogee is a pleasant seaside suburb with marine-themed street names and a variety of lively pubs and clubs, notably the **Coogee Bay Hotel** (Coogee Bay Road, corner Arden Street, Ph: 02 9665 0000). The nearby suburb of **Randwick** is home to the grand **Royal Hotel**.

Bronte Beach is slightly larger than its neighbouring Tamarama Beach, with a playground, sea pool and more open space. It is a popular weekend venue for picnics and BBQs.

Hallowed Sports

Typical beachside pursuits — such as swimming, surfing and strolling — make up only some of the recreation in this coastal region of Sydney. A long history of sport, involving some passionately supported local football teams (**Bondi United** (league) and **Randwick Rugby** (union)), characterises the area, as does one of Australia's most noted horse-racing venues.

The football fields at **Waverley Oval** and Coogee are good places to witness local matches during the season. Close to **Coogee Oval** is the long-standing **Randwick Rugby Union Club** (102–104 Brook Street Ph: 02 9665 7079), a modern venue and ideal place for dinner and drinks or to rest up after a busy day on the beach.

The much-loved **Royal Randwick Racecourse** (Alison Road, Randwick, Ph: 02 9663 8400) is also nearby, sitting between **Anzac Parade** and the southern edge of **Centennial Parklands** at Alison Road. In early 1833, the Governor of New South Wales dedicated a piece of land on (what was then) Botany Road for a racecourse. Botany Road follows the route of modern-day Anzac Parade and the land used for the racecourse is now famous as an arena for some of the country's richest races.

Tamarama Beach is a tiny beach where beachgoers often prefer sunbathing to swimming.

Left and right: Coogee Beach RSL; Walking in Dunningham Reserve.

Bondi to Coogee Coastal Walk

This gentle and stress-relieving walk is a great way to appreciate the magnificent coastal scenery of the eastern suburbs. It makes a fantastic half-day out, depending on whether or not walkers choose to incorporate a spot of leisurely café culture or swimming along the way.

The walk is part of the longer Eastern Beaches Coastal Walk — the section from Bondi to Coogee is relatively flat, around 6 km long and takes approximately 2 hours to complete at a nice easy pace.

From Bondi the path leads up to MacKenzies Point with good views overlooking North and South Bondi. The walk then takes you on to Tamarama Beach and then to beautiful Bronte Beach, with its surrounding park and sandstone headlands. A detour via Waverley Cemetery takes you to the final resting place of such Aussie luminaries as Henry Lawson, before reaching picturesque Clovelly, Gordons Bay and finally Coogee.

Maroubra

A large area of coastal park overlooks the ocean directly south of Coogee Beach, leading to **Wylie's Baths**. Beyond this lies the isolated residential suburbia of **South Coogee** and the insular beachside suburb of **Maroubra**. Maroubra is linked with the city centre by Anzac Parade, which passes inland though the retail district of **Kingsford** and the university-oriented suburb of **Kensington**. The **University of New South Wales** (lies opposite the National Institute of Dramatic Art (**NIDA**) on Anzac Parade between **Barker** and **High Streets**.

Maroubra Beach has a popular skate park, rock pool and several notable waterfront structures, including the **Pavilion Café** and two surf lifesaving clubhouses. The name *Maroubra* is derived from an Aboriginal word meaning "like thunder", describing the pounding sound of waves against the beach's shoreline. The **South Maroubra Shopping Complex** is the major retail outlet and, at its rear (400 m from the beachfront), sits the **Sands Hotel** (32–40 Curtin Crescent, Maroubra, Ph: 02 9661 5953), which povides Maroubra's main tourist accommodation. **Pacific Fair**, at Maroubra Junction, is the other major shopping centre in this suburb.

Top to bottom: **Bali Bombing Memorial, Coogee** A reminder of the 20 people from the eastern suburbs of Sydney who lost their lives; **Beach showers** help to rinse off the sea salt after a day in the surf.

Left and right: **Maroubra Beach** The Maroubra beach shoreline, roughly 1 km long and four beaches south of Bondi, is only 10 km from Sydney's city centre.

Clovelly Beach to Maroubra Walk

Another great journey of discovery is the pleasant, signposted walk from Clovelly Beach to Maroubra. The walk passes several parks as well as these beaches. Start at the coastal Waverley Cemetery, passing Clovelly Beach into Gordon's Bay and Coogee. Then continue onto Maroubra Beach via Grant Reserve, Trenerry Reserve and Lurline Bay.

Top to bottom: **Balmain War Memorial; Dawn Fraser Swimming Pool, Balmain,** has been popular with the Balmain community since 1883.

The Dawn Fraser Swimming Pool

The Dawn Fraser Swimming Pool is named after the club's most famous member and Balmain resident, Dawn Fraser. A gold-medal winner in three Olympic Games, Fraser's swimming career began at this very pool. The pool is considered important for its historic contribution to the development of recreational and competitive water polo and swimming in Australia. Since 1884 it has also had associations with the Balmain Amateur Swimming and Life Saving Club — the oldest active swimming club in Australia. One of the few surviving tidal public baths (once common in Sydney Harbour), the Dawn Fraser Swimming Pool is the only one to have retained most of its original architecture, created from 1904–24 and demonstrating the characteristics of early 20th-century public baths.

Glebe Markets operate every Saturday and have decorative homewares, new and second-hand clothing, arts and crafts and live jazz entertainment.

To the West

Glebe and Balmain

The suburbs of **Glebe** and **Balmain** are popular for wining and dining, both having a relaxed village-like feel. A stroll through these old, but now rejuvenated, Sydney suburbs is well worthwhile.

Balmain seems purpose-built for casual strollers and window shoppers and much that is of interest to the visitor is found within Balmain's city streets, particularly some fine old pubs and history-rich walking tours. Both Balmain and Glebe are within reasonable proximity to the Sydney Harbour foreshores. Both also have popular weekend markets for bargain hunters and lovers of second-hand collectibles and bric-a-brac. Balmain's **weekend market** is held in the local churchyard, with Glebe's being hosted in the local schoolyard on **Glebe Point Road.** Balmain is one of Australia's oldest working-class suburbs and, in common with many inner-city areas of Sydney, has been through a rebirth in recent years, making it one of the city's trendiest, most affluent suburbs.

As a harbour suburb, Balmain can be reached via ferry. The service takes travellers to Darling Street, one of the suburb's main thoroughfares just a short walk from the suburb's heartland. Balmain was, in its earlier days, the construction site for many of Sydney's now-ageing harbour ferries.

Clockwise from top left: **Balmain Public School; Balmain Glasshouse; Exchange Hotel; Orange Peel Café** Various examples of the architecture on display around Balmain.

Some of the "Locals"

The charm of the suburb has attracted many creative types, including many of the country's most noted writers and artists. The always-popular local **Balmain Historic Pub Tour** not only provides the opportunity to sample fine ales, but also to explore some of Sydney's oldest venues. The tour is held every Saturday (Ph: 13 2077). Some of the favourite "locals" to see include **The London Hotel, The Commercial Hotel, The Cat and Fiddle** (a popular live music venue), the **Sir William Wallace, The Royal Oak Hotel,** and **The Riverview**. For teetotallers, there are plenty of coffee houses and restaurants scattered throughout Balmain.

Leichhardt and Newtown

Sydney's fast-paced lifestyle is facilitated by the city's commitment to caffeine intake. **Norton Street** in inner-city **Leichhardt** is one of inner Sydney's café havens and supports a variety of relaxed outdoor restaurants that are ideal spots to sit and watch the world go by.

Left to right: **Shops in the old St George's Hall, King Street, which was built in 1887; The corner of King Street and Wilson Street, Newtown.**

The equally busy **Italian Forum** is an open-air shopping centre that reflects the areas cultural diversity and European influences.

Another area of inner Sydney that is packed with eateries is **Newtown's King Street,** south of the **University of Sydney.** It is one of the preferred locales for Sydney's alternative hoards and is also a popular place with students.

King Street is now one of Sydney's hippest nightlife districts and seemingly every second business is a bar, nightclub or restaurant. The popularity of Newtown is seen in its busy roadways and side streets, often congested with cars and pedestrians, especially at night.

A significant number of Newtown's venues now hold late licenses, befitting an area recognised as one of Sydney's prime entertainment districts. Popular pubs here include the two-storey **"Marly" (Marlborough Hotel)** the chic **Zanzi Bar,** decorated in exotic tones reminiscent of sultry faraway places, and the shadowy **Kuleto's,** a beautifully retro-styled cocktail bar with tempting house specials.

Modern Newtown is something of a melting pot of ages, socio-economic brackets and varying lifestyles — home to everyone from busy executives (who enjoy its proximity to the CBD) to dreadlocked university students happily operating on "island time".

Away from the buzz of King Street several quiet residential suburbs (characterised by quaint old terrace houses and tree-lined streets) can be found — **Erskineville, Enmore** and **Camperdown.** The pretty parkland at **Camperdown Memorial Rest Park,** next to the beautiful and historic **St Stephen's Church,** is a relaxing old churchyard off King Street that provides a pleasant respite from the main street's crowds. With its fondness for all things exotic, **King Street South,** beyond Newtown Rail Station, contains a more quirky selection of small businesses and specialist retailers. The window shopping along this intriguing stretch of road is always exceptional.

Top and bottom: **Shops lining King Street South in Newtown.**

The Newtown Festival

Dreadlocks and body piercings are strictly de rigueur for attendees at the annual Newtown Festival held in Camperdown Memorial Rest Park next to St Stephen's Church. Street artists, bands, stall holders and locals come together to spend a day in the sunshine celebrating their suburb's quirky uniqueness.

The date each year varies, but the festival is generally held in November and is organised by Newtown Neighbourhood Centre (opposite Newtown Train station at the Old Town Hall, 1 Bedford Street, Newtown, Ph: 02 9516 4755).

The Italian Forum, Leichhardt If you are a lover of good pasta, exceptional coffee, glorious gelati and quality fresh produce, then the Italian Forum is the place for you. With a fantastic selection of Italian gourmet delights, many will think themselves transported to the Mediterranean.

Italian Treats

Enjoy an Italian pastry at Mezzapica or the finest hand-blended roasted coffees at Caffe Bianchi.

Fine dine at one of the multi-award winning restaurants: Elio and Grappa.

Sydney by Cycle

Homebush Bay and its surrounding local areas are linked by an extensive network of cycleways. With distinctive signposting, they allow visitors a safe cruise. RTA Motor Registries (Ph: 1800 060 607) provide detailed cycleway maps of the area for cycling enthusiasts.

Home of Sports

Olympic Park at **Homebush Bay**, considered the geographical centre of modern Sydney, was the main site for Sydney's phenomenally successful 2000 Olympic Games. The site, served by the purpose-built Olympic Park train station, contains sporting arenas and venues for facilitating major events, including its colossal centrepiece, **Telstra Stadium**. Sydney Olympic Park is also the home of the **Sydney Showground**, which accommodates the hugely popular Royal Easter Show. The precinct contains many pleasant walks and parks including the dramatic "glass pyramid" hilltop at the western end of the site.

Overall, Olympic Park resembles a suburb totally dedicated to sports and recreation. Various monuments and memorials devoted to the Sydney Games can be found throughout the precinct. All of the sports facilities in the park are still in use on a daily basis. For relaxed sports-free sightseeing, **Bicentennial Park** and the **Millennium Parklands** are the preferred spots.

Although the Olympic Park precinct covers a large area, most sections are easily accessed by foot from the train station and the main roadway through Olympic Park: **Olympic Boulevard**. Olympic Park is also accessible by ferry from **Circular Quay**. The service travels along Parramatta River to Olympic Park Ferry Wharf.

Direct Factory Outlets

Although it is not generally considered a retail area, Homebush Bay is the home of DFO (Direct Factory Outlets, Ph: 02 9748 9800), an undisputed mecca among bargain hunters seeking out discounted brand-name apparel. With fantastic prices, and a range of goods from Ugg Boots® to berets, DFO is well worth a look (or a guilt-free splurge) when in this area.

Rosehill Gardens Racecourse

The Aussie love of a flutter is given free "rein" at Rosehill Gardens. This distinguished race track hosts a number of prestige events, including the Sydney Turf Club's annual showpiece and the world's richest horse race for two-year-olds — the Golden Slipper. Ever since Todman's legendary victory in 1957, the "Slipper" has attracted the cream of Australia's racing fraternity. It has also become something of a style exposé — a favoured occasion for female punters keen to flaunt the best in exclusive Sydney fashion and millinery.

Rosehill's splendid racecourse is encircled by expanses of manicured lawn, beautifully landscaped gardens and artistic floral displays. Rosehill boasts excellent modern facilities, catering to both members and casual visitors, and is a superior venue for the "sport of kings".

Top to bottom: **Bicentennial Park; Olympic Park; Sculpture at Sydney Olympic Park; Rosehill Gardens.**

Parramatta

Parramatta is one of Sydney's busiest centres and a region in which there is much to savour. A city within greater metropolitan Sydney, it has a long colonial history and a contemporary workaday vibe as well. Situated in the heartland of Sydney's western suburbs, Parramatta is accessible from central Sydney by both train and ferry. The hour-long ferry ride from Circular Quay takes in the sunny Parramatta River and its attractive shoreline suburbs.

The **Parramatta Heritage and Visitors Information Centre** (346A Church Street, Parramatta, Ph: 02 8839 3300), overlooking Parramatta River and the convict-built **Lennox Bridge,** is a good place to begin a discovery of this old district of Sydney. Parramatta lies just 24 km from the Sydney CBD and 6 km from Olympic Park at Homebush Bay.

Experiment Farm Cottage takes visitors back to the first years of European settlement in New South Wales.

Clockwise from top: Aerial view of Parramatta; Rivercats run from Circular Quay to Parramatta; Riverside Theatre, corner of Market and Church Streets.

History Preserved

Sites of interest around Parramatta include ex-convict James Ruse's first private farm in Australia, **Experiment Farm** (9 Ruse Street, Parramatta, Ph: 02 9635 5655), established in 1791, and **Old Government House,** built by Governors John Hunter and Lachlan Macquarie between 1799 and 1818. Australia's oldest surviving public building, **Elizabeth Farm** (70 Alice Street, Rose Hill, Ph: 9635 9488) is among the country's most important historic sites and contains part of the oldest European building in Australia. From 1793–1850 it was the residence of noted pastoralists John and Elizabeth MacArthur. Now a period house museum, the interiors are furnished with carefully crafted reproductions from that era.

Church Street Mall in central Parramatta also gives visitors the chance to inspect a number of historic structures. Sit in an outdoor café or sample a meal at one of the restaurants surrounded by relics of a bygone era. For the casual visitor to Parramatta, this influence of different periods is perhaps what makes the area so special.

Things to See and Do

1   Visit the Old School House Museum (Ph: 02 9635 8638).

2   Look in Hambledon Cottage, in the grounds of Elizabeth Farm Estate (Ph: 02 9635 6924).

3   Visit Brislington, a museum of medical history of Parramatta (Ph: 02 9843 3106).

4   View Parramatta People and Places, an exhibition of Parramatta's history, held at the Heritage Centre (Ph: 02 8839 3311).

Parramatta's European settlement and establishment occurred less than a year after the First Fleet's arrival. The name *Parramatta* is derived from an Aboriginal word meaning "place of many eels". In keeping with its moniker, Parramatta today is home to one of Sydney's most fervently supported rugby teams, the Parramatta Eels. The river blends saltwater and freshwater in tidal reaches towards Sydney Harbour and contains a healthy mix of nutrients that make it hospitable to the many slippery residents that call it home.

The Geographical Heart of Metropolitan Sydney

Spanning outwards from the busy transport hub of the Parramatta train station and bus terminus at Argyle and Darcy Streets, modern Parramatta's combination of industrious high-rise landscapes, superb shopping opportunities and relaxed suburban living are an ideal counterpoint to central Sydney's more hectic pace, and Parramatta is now understandably popular for these reasons. Many Sydney businesses have chosen to locate themselves in Parramatta thanks to its attractive rental prices and well-established local infrastructure. It is sometimes referred to as "Sydney's second Central Business District" for this very reason.

Parramatta's historic and long-standing civic tradition was further enhanced shortly after the beginning of the new millennium. Growth saw the suburb consolidate its reputation as an important State and local government centre — this occurred with the creation of a new Parramatta Transport Interchange and the establishment of Civic Place, the local government precinct. The New South Wales Police Headquarters was also relocated here from its old site on College Street in the Sydney CBD. Retailing in the area also enjoyed a boost thanks to the vast expansion of the Westfield shopping centre and upgrades to local train station facilities.

Clockwise from left: Boer War Memorial; Old Government House; Rangers Cottage and Dairy Cottage, Dairy Precinct. All of these timeless reminders of history are on display in Parramatta Park.

Parramatta Park

As one of the first points of contact between Aborigines and Europeans, Parramatta Park has important value as a cultural heritage site. The park is listed on the Register of the National Estate and the State Heritage Register. Two of Australia's oldest buildings are situated in its grounds — Old Government House and the Dairy Cottage. Parramatta Park has a number of historical "precincts" and memorial sites, including the Boer War Memorial and the Lady Fitzroy Memorial, marking the site where the Governor's wife was killed in a carriage accident en route to a friend's wedding. The park is an important recreational area for residents of the western suburbs and a number of colourful events are hosted here each year.

Lane Cove

Heading back towards the coast, on the opposite side of the Parramatta River, is **Lane Cove National Park**. Just 10 km north-west of the city centre, it is one of Sydney's more accessible national parks. Here, the Lane Cove River runs along a bushland valley, extending from **East Ryde** to **Wahroonga** and **Pennant Hills.** The park is a hub of visitor activity, where you can also visit the **Kukundi Wildlife Shelter,** take a stroll along the bank, or hire a row boat. There are also many picnic spots, several overnight cabins and a campsite at the nearby caravan park.

Lane Cove National Park has several walks, including the **Riverside Walk** and **Heritage Walk** and the initial section (27 km) of the **Great North Walk** — the lengthy 250 km trek that begins at Sydney Harbour and extends all the way to Newcastle. Information on all park activities can be obtained from the park's information centre (Lady Game Drive, Chatswood, Ph: 02 9412 1811). Lane Cove National park has ample tourist facilities, including the popular **Davidson Picnic Area**, centred on the park's Middle Harbour area and a great place for boating and fishing.

Cyclists can enjoy any of the great trails in the upper Lane Cover River Valley. They can also travel through the park from Lane Cove Road to Lady Game Drive on the sealed road, which is free from traffic and an enjoyable 5 km in length. Large areas of the park were heavily burnt or destroyed during the severe Australian bushfire seasons in the mid 1990s; however, a diligent volunteer program, along with National Parks and Wildlife Service efforts, has helped ensure the park's safe regeneration. There is also a group, **Friends of Lane Cove National Park**, who are enthusiastic and active in their conservation of the area. Bushwalkers can once again admire the local scenery along an extensive network of walking tracks; the heavy vegetation and healthy plant life of the park makes it easy for the visitor to forget they are a mere dozen kilometres from Sydney's city centre.

Clockwise from top left: **Walking through Lane Cove National Park; The Weir; People relaxing by Lane Cove River; The Great North Walk starting point** For a day out, this park is a fantastic option. Go for a bushwalk, casual bike ride or relax in the beautiful surrounds.

Prior to the arrival of European settlers, the park's waterways and estuaries provided oysters, fish, crabs and waterfowl for local Aborigines, while the wooded areas bestowed regular bounties of possum and kangaroo meat. A number of Aboriginal groups embraced these natural gifts prior to 1788. Indications of Indigenous inhabitation in the region include fine examples of rock carvings and drawings. Carvings and axe-grinding grooves can still be found near Carters Creek. Near Browns Waterhole, at the western edge of the park, is a carved track of wallaby imprints. The early history of the park's area after European settlement indicates that the Lane Cove River was a good timber source. The river also provided a thoroughfare for water-borne transport — wharves were soon constructed along the river, including one notable construction by Joseph Fidden (an ex-convict) in what is now known as **Fiddens Wharf Reserve**. A vineyard was also established early in the 19th century in the modern day **Fullers Park** area and other orchards soon flourished in this fertile region.

Wildlife of Lane Cove National Park

Intersected by the picturesque Lane Cove River, this urban "menagerie" comprises 600 ha of peaceful forest and marshland that is home to an interesting variety of native fauna. Birds are attracted to the woodland areas. Rainbow Lorikeets are common, congregating on eucalypt branches in boisterous clans. Tawny Frogmouths, with their excellent camouflage and nocturnal habits, can easily pass unnoticed. Some of the more unusual mammalian residents are Short-beaked Echidnas, Sugar Gliders and Swamp Wallabies. Flying foxes gather in large colonies in the mangroves. Reptiles are also prevalent in Lane Cove. Along the river, the Eastern Water Dragon can be spied, often soaking up sunshine on the banks. When threatened, these dragons quickly take to the water where they display their remarkable swimming skills.

Left to right: Grey-headed flying Fox; Eastern Water Dragon; Rainbow Lorikeet; Tawny Frogmouth. These are just a few of the many bird and animal species found in the woodlands around Sydney Harbour.

Admiralty House The tale of
the once naval Commander-in-
Chief's home, now that of the
Governor General, is depicted
in its stained-glass windows.

**View of the Sydney Harbour
Bridge,** from Neutral Bay.

Northern Harbourside

Across the wide span of Sydney Harbour Bridge lies the **North Sydney** business district, characterised by its modern skyscrapers, and home to some of Sydney's most exclusive suburbs.

Kirribilli, on the eastern side of the Bridge's northern end, is the Prime Minister's Sydney base with picture-perfect views across the waters to Circular Quay, the Sydney skyline and the Opera House.

Luna Park

On the western side of the Harbour Bridge is Luna Park (1 Olympic Drive, Milsons Point, Ph: 02 9033 7676), the long-standing fun park instantly recognisable by the massive "smiley face" entrance.

With free entry and stunning harbour views, Luna Park is an ideal place to visit. The energetic can get here by walking across **Sydney Harbour Bridge** to North Sydney's **Milsons Point** and following **Alfred Street** back down to the waters edge, where Luna Park can be found adjacent to **North Sydney Olympic Swimming Pool**. Entrance to the park is through the famous (and somewhat macabre) smiling clown

Luna Park entrance Guaranteed fun awaits kids and adults beyond this iconic facade.

face — its toothy gape nestled between two castle-like turrets. Inside, a variety of rides and attractions keep the crowds entertained. By night the park looks particularly attractive thanks to its illuminated structures. The park has experienced changing fortunes over the years, including a lengthy period during the 1980s when it was closed after fire broke out in its "ghost train" ride in 1979.

Around the Harbour's Edge

Those close to the harbour waters are well served by ferry services from Circular Quay. **Mosman** is one of the most exclusive of the lower north shore suburbs and is a popular place for designer shopping.

Aerial of North Sydney with Luna Park in the foreground The Park allows visitors to take to the Dodgem Cars, Tumblebug, Ferris Wheel and Tango with a spectacular view of Harbour Bridge.

Taronga Zoo

Clockwise from top right: Giraffes have some of the best views of Sydney's CBD; Mountain Goats; The entrance building has heritage significance.

Officially opened in 1916, Taronga Zoo is situated in the heart of Sydney on 28 ha of foreshore bushland. It is home to over 2600 individual animals, made up of more than 340 different species. Australia's most famous zoo plays an important role in the research and conservation of threatened species worldwide, providing world-class habitats and care for these animals.

Cremorne Point is also a spectacular **North Shore** spot — the views back towards the CBD are superb. Directly north of Mosman sits **Spit Junction**, **Balmoral** and **The Spit**, all close to the water's edge. These places have a sunny and relaxed coastal feel about them and are all well situated around Middle Harbour. A walking discovery tour of the area can be undertaken along the **Cremorne** to **Mosman Bay Track**. This path leads through well-maintained gardens that have pleasant water views. Along the way, you'll pass **Robertsons Point**, where you'll get a glimpse of some of Sydney's most famous landmarks. From **Bradleys Head** through **Sirius Park**, via **Reid Park** in Mosman to the end of Cremorne Point, visitors will walk past the **Taronga Zoo Wharf**. The **Taronga Zoo Wharf** is itself a worthwhile starting point for any walks in this area.

Balmoral is a hidden delight on **Middle Harbour**, off Sydney Harbour, away from the more crowded tourist attractions. Reached via Mosman or by water from Circular Quay, it has a small marina, beach, and pleasant parklands. A special feature is the small island which separates **Balmoral Beach** from **Edwards Beach,** accessible by a stone footbridge. The island is an ideal place to picnic. Balmoral Beach is a very popular beach for swimming and for enjoying a walk along the water's edge.

Clockwise from top left: **Enjoying a day out at Balmoral Beach; Aerial of Wyargine Point to Balmoral; Bathers' Pavilion at Balmoral Beach.**

Greater Sydney

With the Pacific Ocean to its east, central Sydney is surrounded to the north, south and west by spectacular national parks and beautiful coastlines. There is a variety of outdoor activities for the energetic visitor to take part in. Sydney's north shore contains leafy upmarket suburbs and many miles of superb surfing beaches leading up to the natural delights of Palm Beach, Broken Bay, Bouddi National Park and the Hawkesbury River.

Australian Pelican

Beautiful Beaches

One of Sydney's best natural assets is the long stretch of northern beaches beckoning visitors to take to the water and indulge in their preferred watersport. From the popular strip of Manly Beach to Palm Beach, where beach lies on both sides of the peninsula that separates Pittwater from the ocean, there is plenty of outdoor fun to enjoy. Take to the gentle lagoons and lush sandy shores of Freshwater, Newport, Mona Vale and Dee Why, all within easy reach and offering so many activities for both the energetic and more laid-back visitor.

Daytrips

For the holiday-maker in Sydney, the city's geographical layout means that there is a multitude of daytrips and attractions in every direction, radiating out from the centre of town. The possibilities range from casual bushwalking and guided tours through to extreme sports such as hang-gliding. Sydney's incomparable location on Australia's sunny eastern seaboard will reward imaginative and adventurous souls with an almost unlimited checklist of memorable activities and attractions.

Back to Nature

The numerous national parks scattered throughout the Greater Sydney region have formed a bushwalking paradise. **Ku-ring-gai Chase National Park** lies on Sydney's northernmost outskirts. Across the other side of the Hawkesbury are **Brisbane Water** and **Bouddi National Parks**, with **Marramarra National Park** to the west. This vast and largely untouched wilderness is just a short car trip away from the CBD.

Ku-ring-gai Chase National Park Wilderness at the edge of the northern suburbs.

Take to the Water

The soothing flow of the tide, the sweet songs of native birds and the cool breezes that blow through the tree-lined banks of the **Hawkesbury River** are all great reasons to take to the water. The Hawkesbury is the perfect setting for a houseboat cruise or a relaxing fishing expedition in search of popular species such as flathead, bass or bream. Whatever the reason, this part of Sydney cries out for visitors to enjoy the natural beauty of its surrounds.

Top to bottom: **Manly Cove; Barrenjoey Lighthouse; Nepean Gorge; St George Regional Museum, Hurstville.**

Royal National Park The splendid scenery in this park features sandy beaches, deep river gorges and heath-covered plateaus.

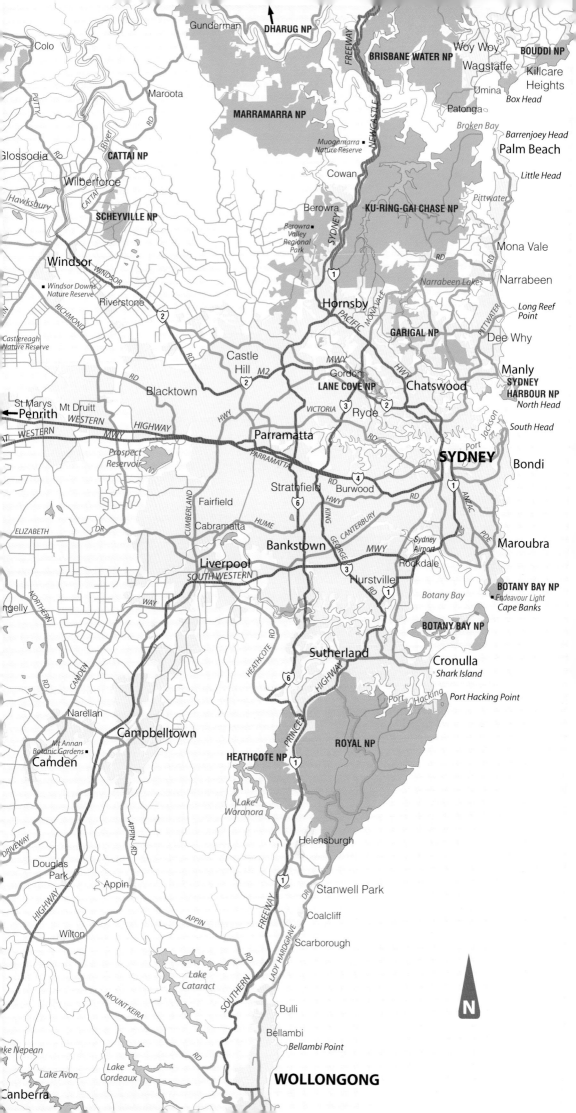

Top to bottom: **Rock Baths at Fairy Bower, Cabbage Tree Bay; Flags fly at Manly Beach.**

Days at the Beach

Beyond Sydney Harbour Bridge lies the radiant stretch of Sydney's northern suburbs and their beaches. Here is some of Sydney's most exclusive and prized real estate. Despite the city's size, the northern beaches remain relatively secluded when compared to the eastern suburbs beaches. Many beaches on Sydney's north shore can be reached by ferry, especially the popular **Manly Beach** — the northern suburbs' rival to eastern Sydney's beloved Bondi.

Manly

The name Manly was bestowed on this area in 1788 by Captain Arthur Phillip in tribute to the bravery he admired in the men of the local Cannalgal and Kayimai tribes. Today, the wide promenade of Manly Beach is graced by a series of stately Norfolk pine trees running along **South Steyne**. The southernmost end marks the position of the attractive **Cabbage Tree Bay**, which is a marine reserve between Manly and Shelly Beaches.

Above: **Looking over Manly towards North Head, site of the North Head Army Barracks.**

Head out for a Walk

Visitors can take the **Cabbage Tree Coastal Walk** to get a closer look at the area's marine life and at the interesting eco-sculptures along Marine Parade. The walk is made even more enjoyable (and educational) with the help of a brochure describing the origins of Manly's seaside art. Walking further north will lead you to the heart of Manly Beach and then onto **North Steyne** and **Queenscliff Beaches**. For those wishing to break up their walk with some seaside succour, the **Manly Heritage Walk** has some superb picnic spots along its winding paths.

Top to bottom: **Manly Esplanade; Manly Beach.**

Manly to Sydney Ferry

Sydney's much-loved ferries have served the city's residents for almost 150 years, running between Circular Quay and the wharves on Sydney's north shore, stopping along Parramatta River as they head west.
  Painted in their distinctive colour scheme of pastel yellow and green, the ferries travel to over 40 wharves, including Mosman, Manly, Taronga Zoo, Homebush Bay, Parramatta and Darling Harbour (among others). Sydney Ferries Corporation also runs sightseeing tours of Sydney Harbour (by day and night) and has day passes to many popular attractions.

The Manly Heritage Walk begins at East Esplanade behind Manly Beach, near the ferry wharf, and continues through to South Steyne. Visitors can complete this walk in a little under three hours.

The other key Manly walk is the **Heart of Manly Heritage Tour**, which circumnavigates the **Corso**. This walk helps visitors to identify places of special interest around Manly, with a strong emphasis on the history of outdoor recreation in the area. **The Manly Visitor Information Centre** on Manly Wharf has further details on these walks and others (Ph: 02 9976 1430).

Shopping and the Sea

Several other urbane attractions dot Manly's beautiful landscape, including the always-crowded **Manly Corso**, a popular shopping and alfresco dining area.

Closer to the Manly ferry wharf (following a relaxed ferry ride from Circular Quay) is **Oceanworld** (Ph: 02 8251 7877), a brief 200 m walk away on sunny **West Esplanade**. Visitors can stroll along a moving walkway that travels through an underwater tunnel. Marine life of all types can be seen here — turtles, sharks, stingrays and plenty of fish. The sharks are hand-fed at 11.15 a.m. and 2 p.m. Also not to be missed are the fur-seals (fed daily at 11.45 a.m., 1.15 p.m. and 3.30 p.m). Anyone with enough stamina can then head over to **Manly Waterworks** (also operated by Oceanworld) where the fun rages on down the barrel of a giant waterslide (Ph: 02 9949 1088).

Fun Festivities

Each year Manly also hosts several major events. The breezy **Manly Jazz Festival** (held every October and considered the home of "Australian Jazz") and the **Manly Food and Wine Fair** both benefit from the suburbs' sunny, beachside location. The food, wine and vibrant entertainment are sure to impress.

Manly Ferry Terminal and Oceanworld
Two great ways to observe the area's watery wonders.

Things to See and Do

1. **North Fort Manly Scenic Drive**
   North Manly
   (Ph: 02 9976 6102)
   The fort includes tunnels, fortifications and the artillery museum. Open Wednesday, Saturday & Sunday 12 p.m. – 4 p.m.

2. **Manly Arts and Craft Markets**
   Sydney Road and Market Lane
   (Ph: 02 9315 8465)
   Open every weekend 10 a.m. – 5 p.m. except public holidays.

3. **Manly Walking Tours**
   7 Cove Avenue
   (Ph: 02 9977 0157)

Top to bottom: Manly Corso; Manly Wharf, Manly Cove With over 80 restaurants in the area, visitors are sure to find a scrumptious meal to suit their tastes.

Art and Adventure

Also popular with visitors and locals is the **Manly Art Gallery and Museum** (on West Esplanade near Manly Wharf, Ph: 02 9949 2435, open Tuesday to Saturday, 10 a.m. – 5 p.m.). Opened in 1930, it was the first metropolitan regional gallery in New South Wales. Since then the gallery has become a cultural talking-point, attracting thousands of visitors every year.

For a more adrenaline-packed tour try **Epic Surf Adventures** (www.epicsurf.com.au Ph: 02 8900 1018) and their thrilling "Waverider" boat rides — blasting passengers across the water at heart-pumping speeds up to 45 knots. These tours take in some of Sydney's most dramatic sections of coastline.

Top to bottom: **Dee Why Head and Curl Curl Beach; Narrabeen Lakes; Para-gliding at Mona Vale.**

To Palm Beach and Beyond

Manly's reputation as the jewel in the crown of Sydney's northern beaches is well deserved, but there are many other seaside areas that attract their own share of devoted sun-worshippers. North of Manly and **Queenscliff** are the golden sands of **Curl Curl, Dee Why, Collaroy, Narrabeen, Warriewood, Mona Vale, Newport, Avalon** and **Whale Beach**. Far from the city centre, these places impart a relaxed pace reminiscent of classic "bronzed Aussie" beach culture and its great surf lifesaving traditions.

Beyond this stretch of shoreline lies **Palm Beach**, situated on a thin strip of land bounded by the sea and **Pittwater**. Directly north of Palm Beach are **Broken Bay**, the **Hawkesbury River** and **Bouddi National Park**. On the water since 1975, the **Palm Beach Ferry Service** (Suite 22, 1097–1101 Barrenjoey Road, Palm Beach, Ph: 02 9974 2411) operates a variety of boat rides around the local area.

The 40 km strand between Manly and Palm Beach makes this one of Sydney's and Australia's most accessible stretches of coastline. The northern beaches have a long history of surf lifesaving clubs (SLSCs) and weekend carnivals but the area also has many excellent diversions outside the sea's endlessly peeling waves.

Boat hire, scenic flights and nature walks are all popular recreations of the region, and you can survey the scope of the area from **West Head Lookout** in **Ku-Ring-Gai Chase National Park**. The celebrated and long-standing **Barrenjoey Lighthouse** and **Keepers Cottage** offer tours on the first Sunday of each month (Ph: 02 9472 9300 for bookings). Located at the southern side of **Broken Bay** near Palm Beach, this is a fantastic vantage for views of the Pacific Ocean and the area's surrounding national parks.

Surf Lifesaving

Surf lifesaving is an integral part of Australia's beach lifestyle. From humble beginnings, surf lifesaving now has some 260 clubs around Australia. In New South Wales, 50,000 members at 129 clubs protect about 1600 km of shoreline. The origins and growth of surf lifesaving can be traced back to Manly Beach, 1902, when William Gocher defied local laws by swimming during daylight hours. Similar actions by others forced the recognition of daylight bathing and surfing, gradually giving these pastimes a prominent place in Australia's national culture. Soon groups of experienced surfers formed lifesaving bodies to assist swimmers who required rescue from treacherous conditions.

The Bondi Surf Lifesaving Club, established in 1907, pioneered the famous surf reel and line. A notable rescue on Bondi Beach was that of Charlie Smith, a young boy who later went on to become the famous aviator Sir Charles Kingsford Smith, after whom Australia's busiest airport, Kingsford Smith International Airport, is named.

The modern day surf lifesaver acts as public relations officer, database for beach visitor information, safety expert and ambassador for Aussie beach culture. Since official records began in 1949, Surf Lifesaving New South Wales has saved almost a quarter of a million lives. Thanks to these fine volunteers, New South Wales' beaches rate among the safest in the world.

Left to right: **Pittwater; Newport** Pittwater is a protected waterway bordered by Ku-ring-gai Chase National Park. Newport is another superb beach in a string of many that stretch northwards along the peninsula from Bungan Head in the south to Barrenjoey Head.

Left to right: **Avalon; Whale Beach** Avalon Beach is situated between Whale Beach (to the north) and Bigola (to the south). Little Avalon point break at the south end is a surfing hotspot, but is not for beginners or the faint-hearted.

The stunning coastline and tranquil Pittwater area lend themselves to a variety of water activities and the relaxed life on the peninsula makes this spot a special daytrip from central Sydney. Sydney's largest waterfront beer garden at the famous **Newport Arms Hotel** has been quenching the thirst of travellers since 1880 (Kalinya St, Newport, Ph: 02 9997 4900). It is an ideal place to grab a counter lunch and watch the boats drift past.

For picnicking, the serene Pittwater and **Narrabeen Lakes** tempt shoreline ramblers and sun-lovers alike. **Pelican Path** is also well worth a visit; it is near the lake mouth and is good for fishing. **The Coastal Environment Centre**, near the Lakeside Caravan Park at Narrabeen, has displays and a comprehensive library for anyone wanting to learn more about this part of the Sydney coast. Self-guided walking brochures are also available (Ph: 02 9970 6905).

Newport Beach features good surfing conditions, a beautiful reef and many shopping opportunities. **Mona Vale Beach** is popular for more leisurely pursuits, such as golf or fishing. Swimming in the baths that are set in the rock platform, separating Mona Vale Beach to the south and Basin Beach to the north, is also pleasant. "The Basin" is renowned for its great swimming and surfing. **Avalon Beach** is also a popular surfing beach and features the "Indian Head" landmark. These sensational beaches are all patrolled by surf lifesavers during the peak beach seasons of spring and summer. In addition, their close proximity to the city provides a myriad of tourist activities and is a fantastic stepping stone to the wider Sydney area and its many attractions.

Narrabeen Here, beach-goers can indulge in any water activity, including rowing, fishing, swimming, boating, or kayaking. There are also some lovely areas for walking.

Whale Beach The origin of the name is unknown, although it might be associated either with the shape of the northern headland, or the beaching of a whale.

Hawkesbury

On the outskirts of Sydney's northern suburbs and beaches lies **Broken Bay** — the Pacific Ocean's inlet at Palm Beach. From here, Broken Bay leads inland to the wide waterway of the famous **Hawkesbury River.** It is a fine place to immerse yourself in miles of natural beauty and is within easy driving distance (45 minutes) of the city centre.

Milson Island, Hawkesbury was renovated in the 1970s as a multi-purpose getaway. It was previously used as a river trading post, veteran rehabilitation centre and jail.

The dramatic **Lion Island**, off the coast of Middle Head, marks the entry point of Broken Bay and the Hawkesbury River. A journey along the river's entire length would span over 100 km. A diversity of touring opportunities exist, from boat hire and houseboat holidays to 4WD adventure drives, rock-climbing and abseiling. Walking tours, bushwalks and water sports are just some of the activities available to more energetic visitors. Go to **www.nationalparks.nsw.gov.au** for a full list of all the self-guided walks on offer around the **Lion Island Nature Reserve.**

National Parks

An indication of the amount of true wilderness visitors can experience around the Hawkesbury River is reflected in the number of national parks bordering this wide waterway — **Ku-ring-gai Chase National Park** lies to the south, **Marramarra** is to the west and **Bouddi and Brisbane Water National Parks** are found to the north. Every one of these places is less than an hour's drive from central Sydney.

Much of this national park landscape consists of rugged Hawkesbury sandstone. The protected rainforests and woodlands, together with mangrove areas, mudflats and wetlands, form sustainable habitats for a hugely diverse animal and bird population. The region is dotted with popular townships including **Patonga**, **Brooklyn**, **Bobbin Head**, **Berowra Waters**, **Wisemans Ferry**, **Windsor** and **Richmond.**

Villages to Explore

Brooklyn Village in Ku-ring-gai Chase National Park is an hour's drive from Sydney's northern suburbs and is the gateway to the lower Hawkesbury River and Broken Bay. Brooklyn is an ideal point from which to explore the waterway. The scenic railway journey on Sydney's northern railway line to the Hawkesbury River Railway Station, Brooklyn, from Central Station in Sydney takes a little under an hour to complete (Ph: 13 1500 for booking information).

Top to bottom: **Brooklyn; Dharug National Park** Brooklyn is small town on the southern bank of the Hawkesbury River and was established in the 1880s as the base for construction of a bridge linking northern New South Wales to the State's capital by rail. It is named after Brooklyn, New York, also famed for its bridge. Dharug National Park is a fine example of Hawkesbury wilderness.

Natural History of the Hawkesbury River

From its headwaters all the way downstream the Hawkesbury River is flanked by national parks. These protected havens provide safe habitats for native birds and mammals of many species.

One unmistakeable Hawkesbury resident is the male Gang-gang Cockatoo (*top left*). With its wispy, scarlet mask resembling some elaborate disguise from a masquerade ball, it is not hard to imagine this bird standing out in the bush; however, because of its quiet nature (compared to most parrots) and slate-grey feathers, the Gang-gang is often hard to detect in its surroundings. This is also true of the Greater Glider (*top right*). Unlike its vocal possum cousins, the Greater Glider is a silent mammal. Despite being Australia's largest gliding marsupial (the size of a domestic cat), often the only noise that marks its presence is the distant crash of leaves as it glides from tree to tree. Gliding, these animals can cover some truly remarkable distances. Greater Gliders have been observed sailing through the air for more than 100 m. They are best seen at night. Use a torch to catch the brilliant shine of their yellow-white eyes. One animal not so easily overlooked is the Eastern Rosella (*inset right*). With its vivid plumage and high-pitched call, this rosella is readily seen throughout the region in open woodlands.

Coach tours also offer organised visits and depart from a variety of Sydney hotels. For a similar journey, with a dash of adrenaline added to the mix, it is also possible to take sea-plane flights from Rose Bay, in Sydney's eastern suburbs, along the northern beaches up to the Hawkesbury.

River Activities

For an even bigger rush, time your visit to attend the Hawkesbury's celebrated **"Bridge to Bridge"** waterski and jet boat races. Held in November and May each year, the events attract contestants from all over the world who compete in gruelling races from the Hawkesbury River Bridge at Brooklyn to the Hawkesbury River Bridge at Windsor, some 100 km upriver.

Other events include the **Canoe Classic** and the various township festivals held along the river throughout the year (including the **Hawkesbury National Fiddle Festival** and the **Hawkesbury Show**). If you prefer putting yourself to the test rather than watching others compete, a variety of abseiling rock sports, horse riding and motorcycle tours of the region are also on offer.

For casual cruises why not enjoy a morning tea cruise, sunset cocktail cruise, historical cruise, or a simple and relaxing sightseeing sojourn along the magnificent Hawkesbury in the comfort of a chartered houseboat. The Hawkesbury region has half a dozen houseboat operators offering boats with berths accommodating two to twelve passengers. For a cruise with a difference, travel with Australia's last **Riverboat Postman**, visiting isolated communities that still rely on this service for their mail (Ph: 02 4578 4030 for further information).

Top and bottom: **Dharug National Park** is defined by a series of interconnected sandstone ridges and sinuous tributaries. The landscape is divided into two main catchment areas.

Pittwater

At Palm Beach's northern point where it meets the steady flow of **Broken Bay** and then the **Hawkesbury River** heading inland, is the sparkling waterway of Pittwater estuary, winding its way to the south-west. It runs behind the golden shores of Palm Beach, giving the beach a land-bridge or peninsula-like feel.

The Pittwater estuary has many noted suburbs along its eastern banks. On the western shore lies the edge of **Ku-ring-gai Chase National Park.** The estuary of Pittwater itself is a part of Broken Bay. Although quite a hike from the centre of Sydney, Palm Beach and Pittwater – along with Ku-ring-gai Chase National Park – are all worth a visit. A pleasant vista of the region can be viewed from **Observation Point**, at the far northern end of **Barrenjoey Road** in Palm Beach.

The northernmost points of Palm Beach, at Shark Point and Barrenjoey Head, form part of Ku-ring-gai Chase National Park. A portion of this headland is dedicated to the Palm Beach Golf Club (Ph: 02 9974 4079).

Visitor Information

The Pittwater Visitors Information Centre is located within the Mona Vale Library, 1 Park Street (Ph: 02 9997 8717).

It can provide information and brochures on boating, sailing, fishing and cruising. It also has club and restaurant guides, detailed information about accommodation and will keep any visitor well informed about local events.

Maps for bushwalks are also provided.

Top to bottom: **Scotland Island; Barrenjoey** at the tip of the peninsula.

Salt of the Earth

Scotland Island, was originally named Pitt Island by Captain Phillip but was later renamed after the homeland of the original landowner, Andrew Thompson. He ran a successful salt works on the island for many years, extracting, from seawater, up to 90 kg of salt a week.

Situated on the narrow strip of land between Palm Beach and Pittwater, it is an attractive golf course favoured by locals as well as visitors. Its picturesque location where Barrenjoey Lighthouse fronts onto Pittwater makes for superb ocean views.

Another highlight on the waters of Pittwater is the delightful community of **Scotland Island.** In common with the small number of residents living on the western shores of Pittwater, Scotland Island is one of the "Offshore Communities" that enjoy a peaceful and isolated lifestyle in this unique part of Sydney.

Church Point Ferry Service (Ph: 02 9999 3493) connects **Scotland Island's Bell Wharf** with various points around the surrounding mainland, including the youth hostel at **Halls Wharf** and **Church Point**.

Ku-ring-gai Chase National Park

The townships on the western edge of Pittwater all largely front onto Ku-ring-gai Chase National Park. Opened in 1894, this celebrated national park has many miles of meandering creeks and rivers, quiet unpopulated beaches and thick forests. It also conserves Aboriginal history, with special sites and rock engravings situated on the popular **Resolute Track**. There are many activities to enjoy in the park, including horse riding, fishing, swimming, cycling, car touring, walking and camping.

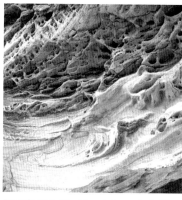

Top to bottom: **Sandstone** is the geological foundation of Ku-ring-gai Chase; **West Head Lookout** affords unsurpassed views.

Popular highlights of Ku-ring-gai Chase National Park include **Bobbin Head** and **The Basin**, the latter being a secluded lagoon and beach favoured by picnickers and families for its safe swimming and attractive location by the Pittwater shores.

Bobbin Head is perhaps the most built-up part of the park, housing an information centre (Ph: 02 9472 8949) and the nearby **Kalkari Visitor Centre**, giving details about the area's nature trails and wildlife sanctuary. Many of the Ku-ring-gai Chase National Park trails lead to Bobbin Head, so it is easily accessible to the visitor. Picnic and swimming spots are also reached from here, as is the park's "Sphinx" statue, much-loved by kids.

A significant number of guided walks (Ph: 02 9472 9300 for information) are available through this massive stretch of wilderness, ranging from easy short walks to longer treks and intriguing night tours. The Resolute Track is a park highlight, taking visitors to spectacular Aboriginal sites, as is the remote north-western part of the park and the spectacular **West Head Lookout** offering some of the best views of the waterways of Broken Bay and Pittwater.

These waterways are, according to many visitors, the national park's most alluring feature. Boating enthusiasts will also find many opportune moments to indulge their favourite pastime, as they will on the Pittwater and Broken Bay waters around the park. There are two marinas within the national park — one at **Akuna Bay** and one at Bobbin Head.

One great way to experience Ku-ring-gai Chase — in a manner truly befitting its colonial heritage — is via horseback. There are over 15 km of trails dedicated to horse riding, taking in the wilderness around **Terrey Hills** and **Duffys Forest** and including sections of the **Perimeter Track**.

Another alternative method for exploration of the park is cycling. The 20 km route from **Mount Colah Station** to **Pymble Station** takes in **Bobbin Head**, the Kalkari Visitor Centre and the Sphinx War Memorial. It provides a good overview of some of Ku-ring-gai Chase's natural attractions and heritage sites.

There is ample wheelchair access around the national park — graded according to varying levels of difficulty.

Right, top to bottom: **Ku-ring-gai Chase National Park; The Basin**, where there is a camping ground near West Head.

The Sphinx

Perhaps looking a little out of place, but much-loved nonetheless, a true highlight of Ku-ring-gai Chase National Park is its 1.5 m replica of Egypt's Great Sphinx. The Sphinx was carved between 1924 and 1926 by a returned serviceman who created it as a memorial to those who died in WWI. The Sphinx can be reached by traversing the Sphinx Track and is a highlight of other park tours and tracks.

Ku-ring-gai Chase National Park Aboriginal Heritage

Aboriginal Associations with the Park Area

Indigenous tribes have an enduring connection with the land of Ku-ring-gai Chase. The cultural and spiritual significance of the area carries the same importance to Aboriginal people today as it did for their ancestors thousands of years ago. The original Indigenous inhabitants were the Gurangai, comprising two separate clans — the Garigal, who lived around the West Head area at the mouth of Broken Bay, and the Terramerragal, who occupied Turramurra's hilly areas further to the south-west. An irreversible disruption to the lives of these people occurred with the arrival of the First Fleet in Sydney. A few weeks after his historic landing, Governor Arthur Phillip began exploring the areas around Broken Bay, making contact with the local Aboriginal people. Within a year smallpox had all but decimated the Gurangai tribes. Farming opened up along the Hawkesbury and white settlements gradually displaced the Aboriginal population. The Gurangai legacy, however, has not been completely lost. This is reflected in the management of the national park, which incorporates more than 800 key Aboriginal sites and works closely with local Indigenous people to protect their cultural heritage.

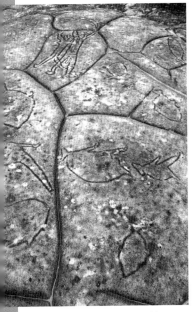

Rock engravings depict earthly creatures and spiritual beings.

Aboriginal Sites in the Park

Sites containing a range of Aboriginal art and anthropological artefacts can be found throughout Ku-ring-gai Chase National Park. There are some excellent guided tours available that take in both the park's natural surrounds and these sites. Visible relics of the park's Aboriginal history include rock engravings, cave art (stencils, paintings and drawings), middens, burial sites, shelters and slabs of local sandstone used for sharpening axes. Rock engravings are a major feature of Ku-ring-gai Chase. The smooth, flat Hawkesbury sandstone has provided the perfect canvas. Much of the art depicts people, animals and god-like beings. Good examples of rock art can be found on the Aboriginal Heritage Walk, The Basin Track, The Resolute Track, and at the Echidna Aboriginal Art Site.

Drawings, paintings and stencils are other interesting artistic features of the park. The most famous of these sites is the Red Hands Cave, which displays amazing ochre hand stencils.

Middens are piles of deposits formed around areas of human habitation and in coastal areas where people fished and gathered shellfish. They usually contain shells, but may also contain animal bones and tools. There are middens located near Bobbin Head on the Sphinx and Warrimoo Tracks.

Midden piles around Ku-ring-gai Chase were probably designated areas for eating and discarding shellfish. The oyster-laden rocks provided local Aborigines with a succulent and ample food supply.

Rocky areas in Ku-ring-gai Chase often display engravings and axe grinding grooves.

The Nature of Ku-ring-gai Chase National Park

Clockwise from top left: Echidna, Platypus, Koala; Spotted-tailed Quoll.

Nearly 30 different species of mammal have been recorded within Ku-ring-gai Chase; however, the majority of these creatures are nocturnal and secretive. Visitors determined to witness first-hand some of Australia's most iconic fauna will need to demonstrate both patience and a light pair of feet. The Short-beaked Echidna will quickly burrow into the soil when threatened. Likewise, the Platypus is easily spooked and will duck underwater at the slightest disturbance. Good times to observe this monotreme are at dusk and dawn. Watch for its distinctive silhouette in any waterway running between steep, vegetated banks (the Platypus prizes such areas for its burrow). Echidnas are best seen during mating season (June–September) when males will congregate in groups around a female. The Koala and Spotted-tailed Quoll are two other animals not easily seen. They are more likely to be located by their voice. Male Koalas have a brash and distinctive bellow. Quolls screech and hiss with intimidating ferocity.

The West

Thanks to a superb public transport and roadway infrastructure, Sydney's wide open spaces beyond the CBD and the city's inner suburbs are readily accessible to locals and visitors alike. Many of the city's earliest roadways were constructed by convict chain gangs, including the immense **Great North Road**, stretching about 240 km between Sydney and the **Hunter Valley**, the latter offering fertile farming lands for settlers, hence its development in colonial days.

Wisemans Ferry, named after ex-convict Solomon Wiseman, who set up the original ferry service.

Convict Contribution

It was apparent during early settlement that a roadway was needed for travel between the Hunter and Sydney. Between 1826 and 1836 the Great North Road was constructed. Newer forms of transport (trains and motorcars) later saw this marvel of early Australian engineering fall somewhat into disrepair, but roadworks were carried out by concerned residents working in conjunction with their local councils.

The road traverses a dozen or more local government areas and parts also come under National Parks and Wildlife Service jurisdiction. Community groups with an interest in its conservation and promotion joined the **Convict Trail Project**, which provides a unique forum for the long-term management of one of Australia's national treasures. In the early 1990s, The Convict Trail Project was initiated by the rural Bucketty and Wollombi communities, concerned by degradation of the Great North Road in their

Nepean Belle on **Nepean River** travels into the gorge and close to the international rowing course at Penrith Lakes.

areas. Similar neglect elsewhere along the Road has seen over 30 working groups join the Convict Trail Project to protect and preserve this historic thoroughfare.

As a result, modern-day visitors can still enjoy its sights. Most of the road continues to be used today, showcasing the beautifully scenic route between Sydney and the Hunter. A self-guided tour brochure is available from the RTA (Roads and Traffic Authority, Ph: 13 1782), as is a self-guided glossy booklet with maps from Tourism NSW (Ph: 02 9931 1111).

Original structural detail such as retaining walls, bridges and buttresses can still be seen on the Great North Road at **Wisemans Ferry** and in Sydney suburbs like **Epping** and **Gladesville**, or in **Dharug** and **Yengo National Parks**.

Nepean Gorge and Nepean River At the foot of the Blue Mountains, the spectacular Nepean River winds its way through the Nepean Gorge. The gorge is found near Mulgoa, south of Penrith.

Left: **Penrith Whitewater Stadium** The perfect outlet for adrenaline junkies.

Penrith Area

Further west is the Penrith area of Sydney's western suburbs and the Nepean River. The river was once a much larger waterway prior to the building of **Warragamba Dam** on the **Warragamba River**, the Nepean's major tributary, intercepting the flow of the waters and limiting the river's size.

The dry, sunny inland climate of Penrith and its surrounds has seen it host some gruelling sporting competitions. The **Penrith Regatta Centre** and **Penrith Whitewater Stadium** (McCarthy's Lane, Cranebrook, Ph: 02 4730 4333) are two well-known arenas for watersports — Penrith Whitewater Stadium being the venue for the canoe and kayak competitions held during the 2000 Olympics.

Nowadays the venue is a popular spot for rafting, beach volleyball and kayaking, attracting both elite and amateur athletes.

The multi-sport triathlon event, consisting of a swim followed by a cycle and run, first came to Australia in the early 1980s and Penrith was one of the first venues to host such an event. One of the country's premier triathlon venues is situated at Castlereagh Road (Ph: 02 4730 6790).

The **Penrith City Council** (601 High Street, Ph: 02 4732 7777) has helpful information on the region and its array of attractions. The **Penrith Valley Heritage Drive** offers the best all-round view of the **Penrith Valley**, its many highlights and history, covering **Penrith**, **St Marys**, **Emu Plains**, the rural **Castlereagh** and **Mulgoa** regions, the **Nepean River** and the **Blue Mountains.**

Featherdale Wildlife Park

Clockwise from top left: Common Wombat; Koala; Dingo; Eastern Quoll.

Another uniquely Australian experience is Featherdale Wildlife Park, where you can hand-feed kangaroos or simply witness Australia's amazing wildlife in a natural bush setting.

Although less than an hour outside central Sydney, Featherdale takes visitors right into the heart of the Australian bush and up-close-and-personal with some of its most popular residents.

The park has a huge Koala colony, Dingos, Tasmanian Devils, wombats and plenty of free ranging and tame kangaroos. There are also amazing aviaries and reptile enclosures. Complete with BBQ and picnic areas and an absorbing nature trail, the park can be found at 217–229 Kildare Road, Doonside (Ph: 02 9622 1644).

South-west Region

The suburbia of Sydney's south-west is a massive sprawl of suburbs stretching out to **Liverpool** and then to **Campbelltown**, the latter featuring some smaller farming lands and horse ranches. Some of these suburbs have become noted for their strong cultural and ethnic influences, such as **Cabramatta**, which lend this area its colourful and cosmopolitan feel. Although there is not a huge number of iconic tourist attractions in this suburban heartland of Sydney, there is certainly a more down-to-earth feel and sense of community.

Cabramatta is home to Sydney's Vietnamese community and offers its visitors many unique shopping and dining experiences. Nearby Liverpool is a noted suburb and an important transport hub, with a thriving and colourful population. **Bankstown** is another important multicultural Sydney suburb, where over 60 different languages are spoken by residents engaged in an active community life.

Above, left and right: **Rouse Hill Estate** is maintained by the Historic Houses Trust.

Important Heritage

Of significant heritage value and offering a glimpse into the home life of Sydneysiders from yesteryear, **Rouse Hill House** (Windsor Road, Rouse Hill, Ph: 02 9627 6777) is situated on farmland in Sydney's rapidly growing north-west.

Constructed between 1813 and 1818 for the free settler Richard Rouse, it has had the longest period of continuous family occupancy of any homestead in Australia.

Rouse was a noted horse breeder and Rouse Hill House included stables with horse boxes named after the famous horses he bred. One such horse, Reprieve, was immortalised in a poem written by A. B. "Banjo" Paterson who visited the house and was inspired by the horses bred there. A descendant, Rodney Rouse Dangar, later bred the racehorse Peter Pan, Melbourne Cup victor in 1932 and 1934.

Part of the collection was recently purchased from descendants of the original owners. In acquiring these objects, Rouse Hill House remains an important part of New South Wales history. The Historic Houses Trust, a statutory authority that is part of the New South Wales Ministry for the Arts, maintains the site.

Tien Hau Buddhist Temple, where visitors can learn about Buddhism.

Temple Treasures

The Tien Hau Temple in Cabramatta (128 Railway Parade, open 9 a.m. – 4 p.m.) was built in 1995 by the Indo-China Chinese Association and is dedicated to the sea goddess Ma Cho, who is believed to have watched over the people on their long journey to Australia from Indo-China. The temple is also a place of worship for Guan Goong, the God of Justice, and Guan Yin, the Goddess of Mercy. A colourful vegetarian feast is held on the 1st and 15th of each lunar month.

Left to right: **A sculpture outside Bankstown Town Hall; Sculptures and elaborate eastern architecture adorn Cabramatta Mall.**

Left to right: **Collingwood House, Liverpool** dates from 1810; **Liverpool Regional Museum** was established in 1989 to preserve and promote Liverpool's history and cultural heritage.

While there, partake of the fascinating "Day Trip to Asia" guided tours or simply soak up the atmosphere amid the suburb's Vietnamese shops, Chinese groceries and Thai herb sellers. It is the ideal way to learn about the exotic fruits, vegetables, meat and ingredients used in Asian cooking, as there are numerous styles of South-East Asian cuisine represented in the area's eateries. Equally intriguing and exotic sites include the **Kwan Yin Buddhist Temple** in Canley Vale (2 Second Avenue, Ph: 02 9726 5713, open everyday 9 a.m. – 5 p.m.), the neighbouring suburb of Cabramatta.

Leacock Regional Park, providing open space at Leacock Lane.

Mt Annan Botanic Gardens

Left to right: Long John Grevillea; Bottlebrush; Acacia in bloom.

Comprising more than 400 ha of native flora and featuring nearly 50,000 individual plants, Mt Annan is the largest botanic garden in the country. The gardens stand as a magnificent testimony to the variety and unusual beauty of Australian vegetation. The park includes feature gardens and pockets of remnant bushland (with ironbarks over 150 years old) and showcases a number of rare and endangered plant species, such as the Wollemi Pine. Some of the highlights of Mt Annan are the Bush Foods Garden, inspired by the D'harawal's (the area's Indigenous inhabitants) traditional use of native plants for both food and medicine, two ornamental lakes and the Federation Flannel Flower Maze. Visitors to Mt Annan will also be able to observe plenty of native fauna, particularly birds.

The Kwan Yin Buddhist Temple was built by the Nung Association, which represents ethnic Chinese from the northern part of Vietnam that borders on China. Dedicated to the Goddess Quan Zin, who is the goddess of kindness, mercy and protection, the temple stands in a tranquil setting of trees and lawn just behind the Canley Vale railway station. Celebrations are held to coincide with the full and half moon of each month.

Visitors looking to venture outdoors can visit **Mount Annan Botanic Gardens** or the attractive **Leacock Regional Park** (south of Liverpool, off the Hume Highway at Casula), which provide wide-open green spaces in Sydney's south-west. The views over the Holsworthy bushland to Sydney's skyline are especially attractive in Leacock Park. In addition, the park's walking trails, along the banks of the **Georges River,** link the park with facilities such as the **Powerhouse Arts Centre** in **Casula** (1 Casula Road, Ph: 02 9824 1121). It is a contemporary multi-arts facility, considered a leading community cultural development organisation. There is also a good lookout platform located here, together with barbecue and picnicking sites. Casula Powerhouse Arts Centre produces and promotes all its own exhibitions, public programs and special events, forming the basis of a National Touring Program that has reached every metropolitan and regional centre in Australia.

Novotel, Brighton-Le-Sands has sweeping views of Botany Bay.

Memorial Square, Hurstville, honouring citizens killed during WWI and WWII.

Top to bottom: **Captain Cook's landing place, Kurnell; Bare Island, La Pérouse.**

Bound for Botany Bay

While the beautiful shores of Botany Bay have retained every bit of the appeal that no doubt first attracted white settlers in 1788, it is a somewhat overlooked aspect of Sydney's tourist attraction trail in modern times. Following white settlement, Botany Bay was initially a rural area where farming occurred and was also one of the favoured locations when colonial Sydneysiders "moved to the country."

To this day there are still some farming lands off **Bestic Street**, one of Botany Bay's main roads running down to the water's edge. The beaches along Botany Bay — **Kyeemagh**, **Brighton-Le-Sands**, **Ramsgate**, and **Lady Robinsons Beach** — are some of Sydney's most beautiful and uncrowded stretches of shoreline.

A visit to Botany Bay is a delightful way to explore Sydney's colonial history and soak up the sunshine. Absolutely stunning views can be enjoyed at **Sydney Kingsford Smith Airport** where its 4 km runway extends dramatically out onto the bay.

There are also a number of other attractive shoreline suburbs surrounding the horseshoe shape of Botany Bay. These include **La Pérouse** (named after the noted French maritime explorer Jean François de Galaup, Comte de La Pérouse, who arrived within a week of the British First Fleet in 1788) and **Yarra Bay**. Wildlife spotters can obtain a close-up look at some of Sydney's shoreline-dwelling birdlife on the secluded nature strip along the bay's Foreshore Road, running in a south-easterly direction from the airport to the Port Botany container terminals.

Macquarie Watchtower at La Pérouse is the oldest structure on the bay's shores and was completed in 1818 to monitor shipping in and out of Botany Bay. **John Cann's** much-loved snake and reptile shows (Ph: 02 9311 3379), on the loop road that marks the end of Anzac Parade and the entry point into Botany Bay National Park at La Pérouse, also continues to enthral visitors on Sunday afternoons.

Top to bottom: **Boatshed Cafe on Frenchmans Bay; Congwong Bay, La Pérouse National Park; John Cann the Snake Man** His famous reptile show has been a popular La Pérouse institution for many years.

Take a Stroll

Other park highlights include the **Banks–Solander Track**, a fascinating 1 km (30 minute) nature trail walk highlighting the species that Captain James Cook's botanists, Joseph Banks and Daniel Solander, collected during their discovery of the area. It begins just a short distance from the Discovery Centre.

Several other notable walking trails are on offer. The **Jennifer Street Boardwalk** is an easy 15 minute stroll through endangered banksia scrub. By contrast, committed hikers can tackle the lengthy 8 km **Cape Baily Coast Walk**, with its deserted heaths and dramatic coastal views.

The 1.5 km **Monument Track** runs between Captain Cook Drive and the Cook Obelisk where James Cook and his crew came ashore.

Botany Bay National Park

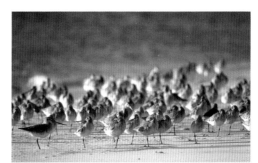

Site of the first contact between Captain James Cook and Australian Aborigines, this area's importance as a wildlife habitat is almost equal to that of its cultural value. Cook's original intention to name the area "Stingray Bay" is an apt reflection of the health of Botany Bay's marine environment. A multitude of fish species thrive in these waters, including the Truncate Coralfish (*below right*).

The area is also a crucial habitat for migratory birds, many of which make their way from lands as far away as Siberia, Alaska, China and Japan. Towra Point Nature Reserve is a low-lying peninsula where intertidal mudflats and sandspits form an ideal sanctuary for over 34 different species of wading bird. Bar-tailed Godwits (*above right*) are common, probing the sand for invertebrates with slender, up-curved beaks. The endangered Green and Golden Bell Frog (*top left*) has also been recorded in Botany Bay National Park.

Further Australian stories of exploration and colonisation are on offer in the **La Pérouse Museum** and the **Discovery Centre** (Ph: 02 9311 3379, open Wednesday to Sunday 10 a.m. – 4. p.m.). A good discovery of the wider local area and its rich history can be found on the **Kurnell Monument Track** with details at Botany Bay National Park (Ph: 02 9668 9111).

Natural Wonders to Enjoy

Bare Island at La Pérouse, **Carter Island Nature Reserve** and the golf courses surrounding the northern headland of the Botany Bay inlet are some of the area's more manicured attractions. Lunch on the waterfront at the **Boatshed Cafe** (1609 Anzac Parade, La Pérouse, Ph: 02 9661 9315) always hits the spot, and at **Yarra Bay 16ft Sailing Club** (Phillip Bay, Yarra Road, Ph: 02 9311 2592) diners can watch the sail boats, windsurfers and kite-surfers on the bay while enjoying a bite to eat.

Heading inland off Botany Bay are the **Cooks River**, running past the airport, and the **Georges River**, heading west past the thriving Sydney suburb of **Hurstville**. Further south lies the comfortable and sunny suburbia of the **Sutherland Shire** or simply the "shire" as its known to Sydneysiders. The area sits beyond the Captain Cook Bridge, ideal to walk across while enjoying the northern view back along the shoreline. Cronulla Beach sits north of Port Hacking and features several beaches along its long stretch of sand. **North Cronulla**, **Elouera** and **Wanda Beach** can be found here, while south of Cronulla proper sits **Shelly Beach**, **Shark Island** and the wide **Port Hacking River**.

Above: Cronulla Cronulla beaches and Port Hacking are both popular for surf or bayside fun.

Camping Sites

1 Bonnie Vale Camping
   Ground — 40 sites
2 North Era Camping
   Ground — 20 sites
3 Uloola Falls Camping
   Ground — 6 sites

Royal National Park

On a clear and haze-free day in central Sydney, the wide green expanses of Royal National Park can be seen from the observation deck of Sydney Tower in the CBD. Situated some 32 km south of Sydney, between **Loftus** and **Stanwell Tops**, it is Australia's oldest national park and the world's second-oldest (after Yellowstone in the USA), having celebrated its 125th birthday in April 2004. Originally named "National Park", it was renamed Royal National Park following a visit in 1954 by Queen Elizabeth.

Royal National Park is readily accessible from Sydney. There are four railway stations (**Engadine**, **Waterfall**, **Heathcote** and **Loftus**) with nearby access to Royal National Park's walking tracks. In-depth park information can be obtained from the National Parks and Wildlife Service (Farnell Avenue, Audley Heights, Ph: 02 9542 0648).

Surfing beaches in Royal National Park include **Garie**, **North Era**, **South Era** and **Burning Palms**, all found along the park's southern coastline. For boating opportunities try the hiring service from Audley Boat shed (Ph: 02 9545 4967), a good place from which to head upstream towards one of several popular picnic spots.

Royal National Park was the starting point for Australia's network of parks and reserves and it remains a popular destination for millions of backpackers, campers, and daytrippers from Sydney and beyond each year. The park contains landscapes ranging from lush Australian bush to coastal escarpments, and protects almost 250 species of animal.

A particularly attractive way of accessing the park is via the ferry from Cronulla to Bundeena. A train service also runs from Sydney's Central Station to Otford.

Chasms in the sandstone cliffs on The Coast Track reveal glimpses of azure waters.

Activities on Offer

Picnic, camping and barbecue areas are available throughout Royal National Park and popular activities include swimming, surfing, canoeing, boating, fishing, cycling and bushwalking.

Many trails make their way to secluded beaches and picnic and camping areas and some are especially popular — including the 8 km trek to the pretty beach at Burning Palms. An elegant, Victorian-era feel is found in the spectacular **Lady Carrington Walk** and at **Audley** where, in 1887, some 3700 ornamental trees were planted. The forests along Lady Carrington Drive, historic trails on the **Hacking River** route and swimming at **Wattamolla** (on the beach or in the lagoon) are other pleasant recreational activities for park visitors to enjoy. There are also **Spotlight Safaris** where visitors can join a ranger and roam the rainforest at night trying to find elusive nocturnal animals like the Eastern Pygmy-possum. Alternatively, discover the source of the mighty Port Hacking River at **Kellys Falls**, with its 48 m drop over cliffs.

Left, top to bottom: **Semi-detached Point and South Era Beach; Wattamolla** is one of the many great swimming locations along Royal National Park's coastline.

Those not afraid to hit the water can also canoe along **Muddy Creek**. This day out allows visitors to paddle downstream to **Grays Point** for morning tea. Kids will enjoy getting up-close-and-personal with yabbies on the Yabbie Dabbie Doo excursion. At the creek they will have a chance to learn more about these amazing freshwater crayfish and also observe eels, spiders and native shrimps. All these ranger-guided walks and activities are wonderful ways to really learn more about this glorious park (Ph: 02 9542 0649).

The **Coast Track,** a two-day walk across 26 km of diverse terrain with spectacular views, is a more hands-on approach to viewing the park's attractions. It provides visitors with an in-depth exploration and discovery tour of the park's distinctive cream-coloured sandstone terrain.

Cycling is another excellent way to explore the scenery of Royal National Park and separate trails have been designed to accommodate this popular activity. The **East Heathcote** and **Loftus Loops Trails** comprise reasonably flat terrain, but also include some steep and challenging sections up rocky fire trails and descending into creek crossings.

The park landscape is one of sheer valley walls, high ridges and rocky outcrops. Its pretty streams are complemented by waterfalls and pools. The local geology is characterised by sandstone rock formed around 200 million years ago when Australia was part of the massive Gondwanaland supercontinent. The Hacking River system has slowly been eroding the sandstone into dramatic gorges over an estimated 50 million years.

Top to bottom: **Audley is a first-class place for** picnics and boating.

Audley

The orderly sense of Victorian outdoors life at Audley, with its expansive, grassy picnic lawns and pretty rowboats, is a highlight of Royal National Park. It is also the oldest area in Royal National Park developed for recreational purposes, and has been a popular place for leisure for more than a century. Its dance hall, picnic pavilion, boat shed and other buildings reflect its historical development over time, as do the ornamental trees and other plants found in the area. Freshwater and saltwater converge at Audley, making it an excellent place to explore by boat — either along **Kangaroo Creek** or the Hacking River.

Top to bottom: **Wattamolla; Experiencing the sights, sounds and smells of the ocean on the sandstone cliffs of The Coastal Walk, between Wattamolla and Curracurrang.**

Heathcote National Park

This park is a treasure trove for enthusiastic bushwalkers. Visitors can enjoy the many habitats found in this rocky reserve and swim in pools hidden within the gorges. Heathcote National Park is part of the traditional land of the Dharawal Aboriginal people. Throughout the park there are engraving sites on sandstone outcrops and shelters featuring pigment art.

The land, waterways, plants and animals are featured in all facets of Aboriginal recreational, ceremonial and spiritual culture. Many plants were used to supplement those traditionally used as main sources of food and medicine. Many of them are also associated with dreaming stories and cultural learning that is still passed on today. The National Parks and Wildlife Service works very closely with local Aboriginal communities to protect the rich heritage found in this beautiful region.

Wildlife of Royal National Park

The sloping sandstone plateau that is Royal National Park is distinguished by many diverse environments packed into a relatively small area. There are a number of geologically unique areas within the park, including cliff-top sand dunes, caves and low coastal ridges in the areas protected by surf. The park itself is a mix of steep valleys, forested ridges, exposed plateaus and rocky outcrops. The Hacking River has forged its way through the sandstone and there are a number of waterfalls, freshwater streams and lagoons throughout. Apart from the beautiful beaches, there are subtropical, warm temperate and coastal rainforests; wet and dry eucalypt forests; heathlands; mangroves; saltmarsh and swamp areas. This wide range of habitats sustains a great variety of native fauna: mammals, birds, reptiles, amphibians, and marine creatures. With over 100 km of walking tracks for visitors to explore, many of the park's inhabitants can be comfortably observed.

Red-necked Wallaby

Mammals

Short-beaked Echidna

More than 40 native mammal species have been recorded in Royal National Park. Mammals inhabit all of the park's environments but are most plentiful in the rainforests and wet sclerophyll forests. Brushtail and ringtail possums enjoy a nocturnal reign high in the treetops, as do Sugar Gliders and the Eastern Pygmy-possum. On the ground small, carnivorous marsupials (such as the Brown and Dusky Antechinus) and native rodents (the Bush Rat) have adapted well to their woodland and dry forest surrounds. Here they forage busily through leaf litter, uncovering a succulent smorgasbord of different grubs and insects. Around the park's waterways visitors may occasionally glimpse Water Rats or Platypuses. One of the park's rarer inhabitants is the Spotted-tailed Quoll, a solitary, night-time hunter that searches for small mammals and birds in a variety of different habitats, both on the ground and in trees. It makes its den in hollow logs and rocky crevices.

Swamp Wallaby   Sugar Glider   Brown Bandicoot

Reptiles and Amphibians

The herpetofauna (reptiles and frogs) of Royal National Park is a rich and fascinating mix. The great variety of these animals is due to both the number of habitats and the favourable climate. Snakes are common, preferring rainforest and moist areas where water is plentiful. There are a number of venomous species including the Red-bellied Black Snake, Southern Death Adder and Tiger Snake. Snakes are naturally shy and not dangerous unless provoked. If a snake is encountered, it should be given enough space to retreat. The park is also home to a healthy population of snakes' preferred prey — frogs. Many frog species are found here, such as the Red-crowned Toadlet and Pobblebonk Frog, and some are even endangered (like the Green and Golden Bell Frog).

Tiger Snake

Red-bellied Black Snake

Lace Monitor   Red-crowned Toadlet   Pobblebonk Frog

Birds and Birdwatching

Royal National Park is home to over 240 different bird species and the great number of excellent walking tracks and vantage points available to visitors make the area a birdwatcher's paradise.

The rainforests contain two of the most intriguing birds in the country — the Satin Bowerbird and the Superb Lyrebird. The Superb Lyrebird is a renowned mimic and a theatrical suitor of females, while the Satin Bowerbird is an accomplished architect, crafting perhaps the most intricate nest of all of the Australian birds. The distinctive call of the Eastern Whipbird is a rainforest catchcry, familiar and comforting to anyone who enters these realms; however, the bird itself is elusive and not readily observed.

In the eucalypt forests, the treetops explode with the raucous screeching and boisterous chatter of rosellas, cockatoos and lorikeets. These are common denizens of the park and are often seen in their noisy flocks during the day. Some of the most striking types of parrot are the Gang-gang Cockatoo, Major Mitchell's Cockatoo and the spectacular Rainbow Lorikeet.

The coastal areas of Royal National Park provide different homes to a number of sea birds. The cliffs shelter gulls and terns and form observation posts for Ospreys and White-bellied Sea Eagles to survey the vast hunting grounds of the Pacific Ocean. The plateaus and coastal heathlands contain banksias and wattles — the perfect food source for inquisitive, nectar-lovers like the New Holland Honeyeater and Red Wattlebird. Below, along the beach and estuarine areas, migratory species such as the Eastern Curlew can be easily observed.

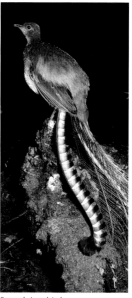

Superb Lyrebird

Female Satin Bowerbird

Wonga Pigeon

New Holland Honeyeater

Diving and Marine Life

Green Moray Eel

With around 30 km of pristine coast, Royal National Park is blessed with a multitude of fantastic dive locations, with more than 100 separate dive sites available for exploration.

Around Port Hacking are some of the most popular areas for diving. **Barrens Hut**, **Marley Head**, **The Balcony**, and **The Split** are all excellent temperate-water dive sites. One of the better reefs is known as **Underwater Wilderness** or **The Gullies**. This site lies around 500 m south of Barrens Hut at a GPS reading of 34° 05′ 40″S 151° 10′ 04″E. The caves and rocky platforms here are home to Port Jackson sharks and numerous rays and wobbegongs. There is also a good variety of colourful sponges and soft corals. Vivid sea stars, like the Carpet Star, strike bold contrasts when set against the sea floor.

Most of the dive sites are distinguished by shelving drop-offs, boulders strewn over rock bottoms, caves and canyons. Some of the more interesting fish to use these places for shelter are the protected Blue Groper and moray eels. Well-camouflaged sea dragons can also be seen by canny divers.

Crimson-banded Wrasse

Pineapplefish

Carpet Star

Weedy Sea Dragon

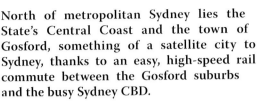

North of Sydney

North of metropolitan Sydney lies the State's Central Coast and the town of Gosford, something of a satellite city to Sydney, thanks to an easy, high-speed rail commute between the Gosford suburbs and the busy Sydney CBD.

Eastern Grey Kangaroo

Surrounding Townships

Further north from Gosford is the historic and active port town of **Newcastle**, recognised for its industry, university, rich heritage, convivial atmosphere and superb beaches. Parts of the coast stretching north from Sydney practically guarantee dolphin and whale sightings — something sure to warm the hearts of even the most hardened travellers. Places like **Port Stephens** have built entire tourist industries around these sea mammals and, combined with the quality of their beaches, make an unforgettable travel destination.

Perfect Parks

Ku-ring-gai Chase and **Brisbane Water National Park** are just two of the many stunning wilderness areas north of Sydney. Brisbane Water contains important Aboriginal engraving sites, while the State's colonial heritage can be traced along the convict-built **Great North Road** in **Yengo National Park**.

Wine Country and Beyond

The **Hunter Valley**, cutting a dramatic swathe through the fertile lands north-west of Newcastle, contains some of Australia's finest vineyards and wineries. The wine country gradually gives way to the **Upper Hunter** region, centred around the historic town of **Singleton** and the vast **Wollemi National Park** — New South Wales' largest wilderness area.

Historic, unhurried towns, secluded beaches and majestic national parks characterise the landscape north of Sydney. The region's larger towns provide comfortable bases from which to launch any number of exciting and memorable forays into this unique area of New South Wales. These places, while conveniently connected to Sydney, have developed their own distinct identities, proving to visitors that life outside the big city can offer experiences as rich and rewarding as those in the metropolitan heartland.

Top to bottom: Terrigal; Pepper Tree Wines, Hunter Valley; Wollemi National Park; Port Stephens.

Newcastle

One of Australia's oldest cities, Newcastle is steeped in history, graced with unique character and blessed with beautiful natural surrounds. The best and easiest way to appreciate the town is by foot, thanks to a number of showcase walks that take in both the city's heritage and its environment.

The Bathers Way, a 5 km coastal walk that takes in Nobbys Headland (*top right*), Glenrock Reserve and the historic coal workings at Burwood Beach, is a popular cultural tour. It is well marked and incorporates information about the city's Indigenous, natural and convict history. The East Heritage Walk presents a number of heritage buildings, including Christ Church Cathedral (*right*) and convict-era houses.

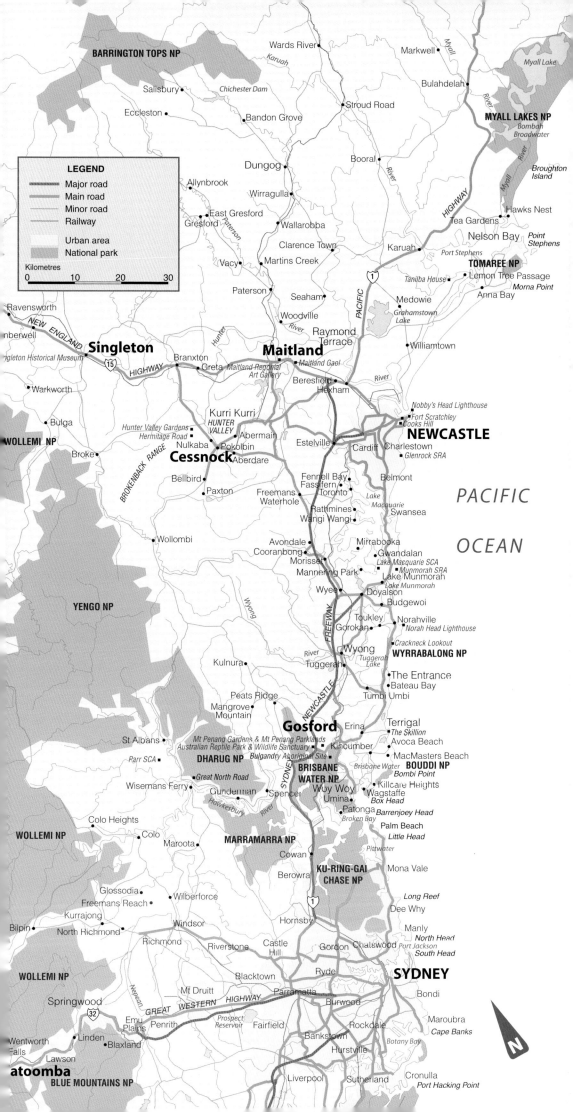

Central Coast

An hour's drive from Sydney is the **Central Coast**, a popular retirement area with plenty of green spaces and long sandy beaches. **Gosford,** only 80 km north of Sydney, has become a viable commute for many Sydney workers wishing to live further afield. **Brisbane Water National Park** lies in this area, together with many significant Aboriginal sites. Around the Central Coast there are also numerous lakes and placid bodies of water, including **Lake Macquarie** and **Tuggerah Lake**, north of Gosford.

Gosford

Gosford is a perfect getaway thanks to its mild climate, nearby beaches, open spaces and good recreational facilities. Farming, fishing, forestry and tourism are key industries to the city's economy. The main visitor information centre (200 Mann Street, Ph: 1800 806 258) is adjacent to the train station. Gosford's town centre is a fairly modern place and has few historical remnants. One exception is the former **Gosford Courthouse**, the oldest building on the Central Coast, designed by colonial architect Mortimer Lewis and built during 1848–49. It is now the **Central Coast Music Conservatorium**.

Pearl Beach is a popular weekend retreat for Sydneysiders with its beautiful beach and appealing range of dining venues. The area also has an easy forest walk through the 4 ha Crommelin Native Arboretum.

Ettalong comes from the Aboriginal word meaning "place for drinking". The beach is a safe place for swimming and its weekend markets have a strong reputation. A novel way to reach Ettalong from Sydney is via the Palm Beach Ferry Service (Ph: 02 9974 2411).

Australian Reptile Park has Australia's largest reptile collection. It also contains a noctarium, areas for milking snakes for antivenes and research, a nature walk, playground and swimming pool.

Henry Kendall Cottage and Historical Museum was built by convicts from local sandstone between 1836–40. Kendall lived here from 1874–75.

Putty Beach in the foreground, looking north-west over Hardys Bay.

Gosford's other main historic sites are the nearby **Christ Church**, built during 1857–58, and the **Henry Kendall Cottage and Historical Museum** (25–27 Henry Kendall Street, Ph: 02 4325 2270, open from 10.00 a.m. – 4.00 p.m. Wednesdays, Saturdays and Sundays). A talented but troubled poet, Kendall served as inspector of State forests, a job given to him by his first publisher, Henry Parkes. The museum retains a few of Kendall's possessions but has generally been filled with items of local history. Also worth the visit is the **Gosford Regional Gallery and Arts Centre** (Ph: 02 4325 0056), which has a beautiful Japanese garden established by Gosford's Japanese sister city, Edogowa. For real history buffs, check out the historic gravestones in the extremely pleasant and tranquil **Pioneer Park**.

Brisbane Water and Bouddi National Park

Right, top to bottom: New Holland Honeyeater; Flannel Flowers.

Less than 20 km from Gosford, these national parks both contain an abundance of native flora and fauna, excellent swimming and fishing spots, and interesting Aboriginal sites.

One of the best sites is at Bulgandry on Woy Woy Road. The Dharruk and Darkinjung tribes occupied parts of Brisbane Water for over 10,000 years and etched engravings into the flat, exposed slabs of Hawkesbury sandstone. The Bouddi Peninsula is the traditional home of the Guringai people, this area also has numerous engravings, middens, rock shelters, and other archeological deposits. Both national parks attract rich birdlife to flowering native plant species such as bottlebrushes.

Top to bottom: **Staples Lookout, Brisbane Water National Park; Bulgandry Aboriginal site.**

Things to See and Do

1 Go to St John Lookout, Katandra Reserve looking out towards Matcham Valley, Erina and the Pacific Ocean.
2 Visit The Fragrant Gardens, 25 Portsmouth Road (Ph: 02 4365 6155).
3 Visit Australian Reptile Park and Wildlife Sanctuary, Somersby (Ph: 02 4340 1146).
4 Enjoy the Mt Penang Gardens (Ph: 1300 304 676).
5 Have fun at Erina Ice World, Erina Fair Shopping Centre (Ph: 02 4367 8244).

Open Spaces to Enjoy

Areas of open space in the region include **Katandra Reserve**, over 50 ha of bushland close to Gosford's city centre, and **Rumbalara Reserve**. These two parklands are joined by the 5 km **Mouat Walk**. Rumbalara Reserve has eight outstanding walks including the **Red Gum Track** leading past a rock shelter said to have once housed migratory Aborigines. Katandra is the more dramatic of the two reserves, with its sheer cliffs and vibrant rainforest, and is best seen on the 1.2 km **Waterman Walk**. This track links with the **Toomeys Walk** that leads up to the **St John Lookout**.

Mourawaring Point (foreground), with McMasters Beach rounding to Copacabana.

Top to bottom: **Maitland Bay; Putty Beach.**

Further Information

Munmorah State Recreational Area
Off Elizabeth Drive,
Lake Munmorah
(Ph: 02 4358 1649)

Lake Macquarie State Conservation Area
Western side of Lake Macquarie
(Ph: 02 4975 1889)

Wyrrabalong National Park
The Entrance Road,
Bateau Bay
(Ph: 02 4324 4911)

Beautiful Surrounds

Between the Hawkesbury River, north of Sydney, and Tuggerah Lake on the Central Coast, are a series of attractive beaches. North of **Bouddi National Park**, **McMasters**, **Avoca**, **Terrigal** and **Bateau Bay** mark the shoreline leading up to **Wyrrabalong National Park**. This stretch of coastline is ideal for all forms of saltwater recreation. The surfing is exceptional, especially around the points at **Avoca** and **Terrigal**.

Avoca

Avoca has become a favoured holiday retreat for wealthy Sydneysiders. The powerful swell and strong rips at north Avoca are for advanced wave riders only. For quieter waters try **Avoca Lake**, behind the beach, a popular place for hiring paddle boats, canoes and surf skis. The **Captain Cook Lookout** has prime views to the south and north beyond Avoca to Terrigal's headland (called **The Skillion**).

Terrigal has a reputation as a good surfing break due to the point at Broken Head.

The Skillion is the narrow, high section of the headland at Terrigal.

Forresters Beach has crystalline water and sweeping shorelines.

Terrigal

Terrigal Beach has a similarly upmarket feel to Avoca due to its irresistible scenery (which includes a line of long-standing Norfolk Pines along the beachfront). Terrigal, 90 km north of Sydney, is one of the most popular tourism and retirement districts. Hang-gliding is a popular pursuit further north at **Forresters Beach**. Beyond Forresters is Bateau Bay and Wyrrabalong National Park, leading to a stretch of popular swimming and surfing beaches — **Blue Lagoon**, **Shelly Beach** and **Toowoon Bay**.

Wyrrabalong National Park

Wyrrabalong is divided into a northern and southern park, each protecting patches of remnant littoral rainforest, but also distinguished by their own unique botanical traits.

North Wyrrabalong features a beautiful open forest of Red Gum growing along its sandy dunes. Interspersed among these impressive trees is a blooming patchwork of banksias, burrawangs, and even cycads (*left*).

South Wyrrabalong has a number of high headlands and rock platforms. False sarsaparilla, she-oaks, and closed heath thrive here.

Picturesque Parks

Wyrrabalong National Park covers some 600 ha and has two main lookouts — **Wyrrabalong Lookout** on the Cromarty Hill cliff edge (with sweeping views to the south), and **Crackneck Lookout**, reached after a pleasant 1.5 km walk through park woodlands.

The track used to reach the lookout continues for another 2 km to Bateau Bay, which features a flourishing population of marine and bird life. Beyond this sits **Lake Macquarie** and the coastal **Munmorah State Recreation Area**. Munmorah offers idyllic ocean views and is a prime place for outdoor pursuits, including camping, bushwalking, surfing and fishing.

Perhaps the Central Coast's most endearing attraction is the Australian Pelican feeding (daily at 3.30 p.m., Ph: 1800 335 377) at Memorial Park, The Entrance. The commentary and the sight of pelicans gorging themselves is an entertaining afternoon for all visitors. **Wandering The Lake Cruises** (The Entrance Jetty, Ph: 1300 737 453) has regular boat tours over the waterways of Tuggerah Lake, **Wyong River** and **Ourimbah Creek**.

Toowoon Bay SLSC surf carnival. **Aerial view of The Entrance** where the ocean meets Tuggerah Lake.

Lake Macquarie

South of Munmorah State Recreation Area is **Lake Munmorah** and to the west is beautiful **Lake Macquarie**. The lake is significant for two reasons; firstly, it is the largest saltwater lake in Australia (indeed, one of the largest in the Southern Hemisphere) and, secondly, its mass and spacious foreshore lends itself to a variety of extra-curricular activities.

Some 16 km of shoreline surrounds this immense, sun-drenched lake, along with lovely bushland — a suitable habitat for its resident population of kangaroos and bird life. Along with nearby beaches, Lake Macquarie is the perfect spot for all kinds of leisure activities, including swimming, cruising, scuba safaris, sailing, long walks and picturesque sightseeing. The pretty, secluded bays and inlets are idyllic all year round. Highlights are **Awaba Bay**, with its walking tracks and areas of regenerated native bushland.

Similarly, a journey into the **Lake Macquarie State Conservation Area** offers visitors the chance to view rainforest gullies and other protected areas. The park's **Gap Creek** and **Dora Creek** lead into Lake Macquarie, and **Monkey Face Lookout** is a great place for visitors to view the area. Rainforest walks lead visitors through towering Flame Trees, Red Cedar and eucalypts.

Clockwise from left: Australian Pelicans resting at Lake Macquarie; Swansea Heads; Glenrock State Reserve.

Newcastle

Newcastle, 170 km north of Sydney, is the second-largest city in New South Wales and Australia's sixth largest city. It has a population of around 250,000 and a proud history as an industrial town (although this has diminished following the closure of BHP Steel in 1999). Newcastle is located at the mouth of the **Hunter River** and has a large and extremely busy port. The city's industrial aspect gives way to pleasant coastal ecology at the city's beaches and a spectacular seaside lookout at **Mount Sugarloaf**.

Harsh History

Lieutenant John Shortland reported coal deposits in the region while pursuing a group of convict escapees in 1797, naming the local river the Hunter after Governor John Hunter. Soon coal was being collected and sold in Sydney.

Aerial of Newcastle showing the city and Nobbys Head (foreground).

In the early 1800s Governor King decided that the site would form an ideal base for a secondary penal colony. The convict settlement was named Newcastle after England's city of the same name. Severe work conditions soon gave the new settlement a fearful reputation.

By 1814, housing over a thousand convicts, Newcastle had become the major prison in New South Wales. Australia's first public school, and a hospital, were erected several years later. The harsh colony was short-lived as settlers moved northwards. Felons were transported to **Port Macquarie** as the Hunter Valley expanded. Nowadays, little of Newcastle's rough beginnings are evident. It is a pleasant, lively city with good beaches and a large university. A key factor in the city's growth was BHP's selection of the city for its steelworks. Opening in 1915, the city soon shifted from coal to steel production and iron smelting. BHP has since phased out its Newcastle operations but the city continues to thrive on many other industries, including retail and education.

Nobbys Beach overlooking Nobbys Head This beach is an ideal place for families to enjoy Newcastle's surf and sun.

The Obelisk Built in 1850, this landmark has survived lightning strikes, the 1989 earthquake and a 1985 reservoir explosion.

Ocean Baths Close to the city centre, these historic baths were opened in 1922. Newcastle is the home of the nation's first ocean baths and there are several others along the coast.

Queen's Wharf is an excellent place to relax and enjoy the activities at Newcastle Harbour, or to take a walk along the landscaped foreshore.

Where History Is Evident

The Newcastle Visitor Information Centre (363 Hunter Street, Ph: 02 4974 2999) is a good place to begin a discovery of the area. Newcastle's busy harbour is complemented by tempting stretches of coastline, a strong collection of recognised art galleries and some classy heritage buildings. Acclaimed Australian artists, including Brett Whitely, Arthur Streeton, William Dobell, Russell Drysdale, Sidney Nolan and Arthur Boyd, have work featured in the 3000-strong collection of the **Newcastle Region Art Gallery** (Laman Street, Ph: 02 4974 5100).

Shortland Wetlands A visit to the Wetlands Centre is a great introduction to one of the most common habitats of the Lower Hunter.

Coastal Walks

Roller-blading, cycling and walking are all fantastic ways to see Newcastle and fill your lungs with healthy doses of fresh ocean air. The city has a number of thoroughfares for its exploration, including walking tracks and cycleways. One of the more challenging routes is the 25 km Yuelarbah Track, which makes up part of the Great North Walk (the historic trading path between Newcastle and Sydney). It takes in various natural and urban features between Lake Macquarie and Newcastle Harbour.

Newcastle Heritage

As the second-oldest city outside Sydney, Newcastle has an impressive range of historical architecture, with no less than six heritage conservation areas found within the city. Cooks Hill contains a number of Victorian terrace houses — distinctive for their cantilevered balconies. Also prominent is detailed wrought iron and classically styled parapets and pediments. The 200-year-old history of the city is evoked in the ornate architecture of Customs House (*left*) and Newcastle Town Hall (*right*).

Newcastle Regional Museum (787 Hunter Sreet, Newcastle West, Ph: 02 4974 1400) houses reminders of the city's colonial and industrial past. Its prime attraction is the **Supernova Science Centre**, where hands-on, interactive science displays are popular with the kids. Working remnants of the city's past can be found along Hunter Street (featuring the **PWD Building, Police Station Museum** and **Post Office**) and at **Customs House** and the **Newcastle Railway Station,** adjacent to each other.

Fort Scratchley, atop a large knoll overlooking Nobbys Beach, the headland and the Hunter River mouth, is another significant historical site. It was at one time the location of **Nobbys Lighthouse**, and played a part in the strategic defence of Newcastle's shipping and coal industries. Designed by Lieutenant-Colonel Peter Scratchley in the 1880s, it was later upgraded in the 20th century.

In 1942, a Japanese submarine attacked Newcastle, which was targeted for its coal port and production. The guns of long-standing Fort Scratchley had been laying in wait for some 65 years at this point and responded with the only shots ever directed at an enemy vessel from the mainland of Australia.

The rock platform below Fort Scratchley houses an ocean-fed pool called the **Soldiers Baths** (built in 1882). The fort itself now serves as the **Newcastle Region Maritime and Military Museum** (Ph: 02 4929 3066, open Tuesday to Sunday each week).

Right, top to bottom: **Fort Scratchley** was constructed in 1882 and is famous for its engagement of Japanese submarines during WWII; **Bar Beach** is one of the most popular beaches; **Stockton Beach** lies just north of Newcastle and south of Fern Bay.

Maitland Gaol

For something decidedly different, visitors to the Hunter region can experience conditions harsher than those endured by the average budget traveller, with a visit to the formidable Maitland Gaol.

Once home to some of the country's most hardened and dangerous criminals, the prison closed in 1998 but guided tours are now available. Visitors who really want to test their nerve may even join spine-tingling night tours and sleep-overs at the prison.

Hungerford Hill, Pokolbin has a new winery and cellar door that pushes the boundaries of architecture and style.

Hunter Valley Vineyard Travel through the countryside and discover boutique vineyards.

Kevin Sobels Wine continues an unbroken Australian wine-making tradition over 150 years old.

Hunter Valley

Wine Country

The New South Wales wine industry is centred around the beautiful **Hunter Valley** and the wineries in this area have given the region's tourism a major boost. Many celebrated and internationally acclaimed vineyards pepper the landscape of this fertile part of Australia, which has the honour of being the country's oldest wine-producing region.

Two hours north of Sydney, the area is broadly divided into seven main centres, including **Cessnock**, **Pokolbin** and **Mount View**. Other centres of interest include **Lovedale**, **Broke Fordwich**, **Wollombi Valley**, and **Rothbury**. Further north is the **Upper Hunter** and **Singleton**.

Years of Experience

The long history of grape-growing and wine-making has bestowed the local wineries with a deep-rooted wisdom of their craft. Over 100 cellar doors and wineries are offset by views of the **Brokenback Range** and the area is imbued with a real sense of tradition. The shopping options are many and art galleries and antiquity dealers trade a range of truly original wares. Charming retro guesthouses, self-contained cottages and B&B establishments offer great accommodation packages. The valley also boasts burgeoning olive and cheese-making industries.

Pottery kilns at Nulkaba north of Cessnock, built in the 1880s.

Viticulture flourishes in the Hunter Valley.

Maitland High Street is lined with civic buildings, stately heritage mansions and elegant old churches.

Exploring the Region

A stroll through the grounds of **Hunter Valley Gardens** makes for a truly captivating outing. Trips to any of the 100 or so wineries (sampling the region's excellent vintages) is not only a great way to meet people, but will no doubt prove itself to be historically illuminating. Likewise, an invigorating, early morning hot-air balloon ride is an equally memorable and worthwhile way to embrace the spirit of the region.

Nestled among the foothills of the Brokenback Ranges in Pokolbin, the **Hunter Valley Gardens** (Broke Road, Pokolbin, Ph: 02 4998 4000) spans over 300 ha and contains 25 ha of display gardens, a lodge and conference centre, an Irish pub, restaurant, BBQ and picnic grounds, kids play area and a chapel. The **Hunter River Country Visitor Information Centre** (Cnr New England Highway and High Street, Maitland, Ph: 02 4931 2800) has comprehensive information on all local attractions, including the city of **Maitland,** one of the major centres in the region. It also arranges **Wine Trail Tours,** which lead tourists and wine lovers through a series of intimate encounters with Hunter Valley wines as they scour the countryside for boutique vineyards.

Maitland

Maitland was settled in 1810 and its diverse economic activities include agriculture, tourism, and mining. Many of the town's buildings (crafted from local sandstone and cedar) lend the area its time-honoured appeal. A recent addition to the local cultural scene is the **Maitland Regional Art Gallery,** housed in a Federation Gothic building in the centre of Maitland, where exhibitions of local artists works are on display.

Hunter Valley Gardens

Located at the base of the Brokenback Ranges in the midst of the region's wine-making heartland is Hunter Valley Gardens. Spanning more than 25 ha, this botanical wonderland incorporates 8 km of walking tracks and showcases twelve visually distinctive feature gardens.

Visitors can survey the magnificence of the grounds from the pergola perched above the 10 m waterfall of the Sunken Garden (*top left*) or make a tranquil sojourn through the Chinese Garden (*top right*) where raked gravel, Gingko trees and decorative bamboo evoke a real sense of eastern mysticism.

Other interesting diversions are the Rose Garden, an olfactory odyssey through a display of over 8000 roses, and the Storybook Garden, which features a fantastic dreamscape inspired by classic nursery rhymes.

Collectors can also scout Central and East Maitland for quality curios, vintage jewellery and precious silver trinkets found within the clusters of antique, bric-a-brac and homeware stores on the **Antique Trail**. The Hunter River Country Visitor Information Centre supplies antique trail maps and detailed information about shopping in the region. A short-drive from Maitland through the rolling hills of the Paterson area is the **Camelot Lavender Farm** (1312 Dungog Rd, Wallarobba, Ph: 02 4995 6166). Here, fans of the oily purple herb can satiate their senses with a range of body and beauty products and sample unique foods from the farm's tea house. Tours of the grounds are also popular, especially with kids who find it almost impossible to resist the allure of a furry llama.

Hunter River Country

The country around Maitland is rich in history and lauded for its delectable local produce. **Hunter River Country** stretches from Newcastle to Singleton (Upper Hunter Valley) in the west, Barrington Tops in the north, and incorporates both the wine country and Watagan Mountains in the south. Among miles of countryside there are many welcome detours. Explorations further afield take in the stunning **Dharug National Park** with its abundant natural wonders, distinctive multi-coloured sandstone landscapes and clear-water tributaries.

Yengo National Park

Yengo National Park (*left*) is an area of plunging gorges, high ridge lines, rugged terrain and swamps. The park, while rich in natural beauty, also preserves some notable heritage sites.

One important monument to the State's colonial history, the Great North Road, stretches 43 km from Wisemans Ferry in the south to Mount Manning in the north.

Built by convicts in the 1830s, the road formed a passage between Sydney and settlements in the Hunter Valley and features beautifully preserved masonry. A two- or three-day walk (or a one-day cycle) will reveal the relics of huge retaining walls, culverts, buttresses and the oldest surviving stone bridges in Australia.

Upper Hunter

The fertile Hunter Valley cuts a dramatic and beautiful path through New South Wales in a north-westerly direction from Newcastle, Maitland and Cessnock. The Upper Hunter is based around several townships including lively **Singleton, Muswellbrook** and **Scone. Barrington Tops National Park** is north of Singleton, while the region's other major reserves, **Wollemi** and **Yengo National Parks,** sit side-by-side separated by **Putty Road.**

The vast **Wollemi National Park**, at almost half a million hectares, is the largest wilderness area in the State. Reminders of the region's Aboriginal inhabitants are evident in scattered art sites, some dating back more than 13,000 years. Steep canyons, cliffs, and thick forest characterise this untamed natural wonder. **Yengo's** rugged wilderness is more suited to four-wheel driving. With a markedly different lifestyle to the pace and congestion of Sydney, only three hours to the south, the region is characterised by rolling foothills, vineyards, rural guesthouses and B&Bs. Horse and cattle studs are also plentiful. An old-fashioned and timeless appeal resonates throughout the entire region.

Singleton

The town of **Singleton** (Singleton Visitor Information Centre, 39 George St, New England Highway, Ph: 02 6571 5888) on the Hunter River is the geographic heart of the Hunter Valley. It boasts the celebrated **Wyndham Estate Winery**, Australia's oldest winery and producer of acclaimed vintage drops.

With an eye to the future, the nearby **Broke Fordwich** area is in a growth phase in its wine production and, despite its relative infancy, has earned accolades both locally and internationally for its boutique wines.

Singleton Street is lined with quaint heritage buildings dating back to the boom period of 1863.

Burdekin Park and Historical Museum The land was donated to the town in 1837, for a market place, by Benjamin Singleton.

The Courthouse, Elizabeth Steet, Singleton was designed in 1868 by James Barnet.

Hermitage Road, off the **New England Highway** between Singleton and Maitland, is great for absorbing vineyards, inland scenery, rural hospitality, local accommodation, fine food and art galleries. A car is the preferred mode of transport here and, although tours are available throughout the Hunter region, the New England Highway is a well-travelled tourist route and perfect for branching out into the region's most popular areas. A good insight into the Upper Hunter's history is available from the **Singleton Historical Museum** in Burdekin Park. Take the **Singleton Town Walk** for a nostalgic tour of the town's proud history.

Mare and Foal Sculpture, Elizabeth Park, Scone This life-sized sculpture was created by Gabriel Sterk.

Scone has 65 world-renowned thoroughbred and stockhorse studs located throughout the area.

Scone

Similarly, **Scone** is a timeless and tree-lined rural town based around agriculture and racehorse breeding. Indeed, Scone is known as "The Horse Capital of Australia". The town also supports cattle and grain farms as well as a healthy dairy industry.

The **Scone Visitor Information Centre** (Corner of Kelly and Susan Street, Ph: 02 6545 1526) educates visitors about the region's attractions and festivities. As the second-largest horse breeding region in the world (after Kentucky, USA), Scone hosts several major festivals each year. A highlight is the much-loved **Scone Horse Festival** each May, with its street parades, rodeo, horse racing (including the illustrious **Scone Cup**), and the six-week **Hunter Horse Expo** (held during September and October).

On the Lookout for Birds?

Lake Glenbawn State Park, accessible from Scone on the New England Highway, is a welcome retreat for birdwatchers. Home to graceful raptors such as the Wedge-tailed Eagle and Australian Kestrel, the park is well-equipped for family outings, with barbecue and picnic areas, cabins and fifteen campsite areas.

Wollemi National Park and the Wollemi Pine

The largest wilderness area in New South Wales, this national park (*bottom right*) is a labyrinth of canyons, chasms and unspoilt forest. The Colo River runs through Wollemi and has carved a tract of long and spectacular gorges. In 1994 a bushwalker chanced upon a grove of strange conifers growing on the sloping ledges of a deep rainforest gorge. Since the discovery, the story of the Wollemi Pine (*top left*) has attained near-mythical proportions. With a 200 million-year-old ancestry, many botanical experts speculate that this living fossil is one of the rarest and oldest plants on the planet. Because of this, the location of the Wollemi grove (comprising fewer than 100 plants) is a closely guarded secret. Propagation, however, has been successful and the pines are now available for sale in specialist Australian nurseries.

Barrington Tops National Park lies to the north of the Hunter region.

The **Parr State Conservation Area**, named after William Parr (an early explorer of the climes north of Sydney) is a hidden gem adjoining Yengo National Park. The conservation area features a rugged landscape of cliffs, gorges, and stark rocky outcrops, observed via walks, guided tours or 4WD discovery treks.

Pretty **Goulburn River National Park**, near the Upper Hunter towns of **Sandy Hollow** and **Mudgee**, follows some 90 km of the winding Goulburn River and comprises a network of caves, sandstone cliffs and broad stretches of sandy riverbanks that are perfect for camping and fishing. Eastern Grey Kangaroos, Emus and Common Wombats all reside in the park.

Barrington Tops NP

This park rises from the remnants of an ancient volcano to altitudes of more than 1500 m. World-Heritage-listed subtropical rainforests vegetate the park's lower valleys, rising to subalpine, sometimes snowy, woodlands. Popular with bushwalkers, Barrington Tops also has a series of short, easy walks.

Port Stephens and Beyond

The beautiful and relaxing waterside region of **Port Stephens**, roughly 220 km north of Sydney, is home to some of Australia's most inspiring scenery and captivating wildlife. During late winter and early spring, visitors to Port Stephens can witness the spectacular site of Humpback Whales on their annual migration north to warmer waters and their subsequent return voyage to the Antarctic. **Nelson Bay** lies to the south of Port Stephens as it heads inland from the ocean, with **Hawks Nest** sitting to the north.

Port Stephens' temperate climate also attracts pods of Bottlenose Dolphins and, unsurprisingly, crowds of water enthusiasts from all around. One good position from which to survey the area is around the historic **Nelson Head Inner Lighthouse**.

Aerial of Port Stephens, with Tomaree Head National Park in the foreground.

Tanilba House, at Tanilba Bay, was built by convicts in 1831.

Situated on Lighthouse Road, Nelson Bay (Ph: 02 4984 9758, open 10 a.m. – 4.45 p.m.), this heritage-listed site incorporates a maritime museum and terraced tearooms.

Equally fascinating is the beautiful **Tanilba House** (32 Caswell Crescent, Tanilba Bay, Ph: 02 4982 4866), built as a family house in the 1830s by Lieutenant William Caswell. The site, open weekends and holidays, offers light lunches and unparalleled views over Port Stephens.

For adrenaline-junkies, the region has a variety of sand dune and 4WD tours, seaplane flights and fishing charters. The pristine marine environments (perfect places for swimming, surfing and scuba diving) are complemented by the dramatic inland scenery of volcanic peaks.

Tomaree National Park

Nowhere is the beauty of this region more evident than in **Tomaree National Park**. **Tomaree Head Lookout** is rated in the top ten of the world's best panoramic vistas. The headland has incredible views of Port Stephens and its coastal scenery.

During WWII, Tomaree Head became Fort Tomaree when Nelson Bay was utilised as a naval centre by the USA under General MacArthur. Tomaree Head was refurbished with radar equipment, gun emplacements and lookout facilities, and the otherwise relaxed atmosphere of the area adopted an altogether more threatening tone when Newcastle Harbour, 70 km to the south, was targeted for attack by the Japanese navy.

Tomaree National Park features wide sandy beaches and awesome headlands rising from the ocean. The park consists of heathlands, sand dunes, forests, bushland and vaulted coastline.

The 2300 ha park also features **Samurai Beach**, fringed by encroaching melaleuca (paperbark) and angophora forest.

The scenery is particularly impressive during its full bloom in spring. The park also provides good rock and beach fishing. It is also possible to walk to **Fingal Bay** and the lighthouse at Point Stephens.

Nelson Bay

Nelson Bay, the largest town on Port Stephens, is located just inside the Port Stephens inlet near South Head, with access to the Pacific Highway. **Raymond Terrace**, nestled at the junction of the Hunter and William Rivers, is the administrative centre of the region.

Above, top and bottom: **Nelson Bay** has a fine marina and natural harbour.

Things to See and Do

1 Visit the Visitor Information Centre, Victoria Parade (Ph: 02 4980 6900).

2 Take a self-guided walk from Dutchmans Bay to Little Beach (brochure at the visitors centre).

3 Take a 4WD tour along the coastal dunes.

4 Take part in Dolphin watching from May–July and September–November on either the Myall River, Broughton Island or the harbour.

5 Visit the markets at Neil Carroll Park, Shoal Bay Road. On the 1st and 3rd Sunday of every month.

Fauna of Port Stephens

Bottom, left to right: Osprey; Point Stephens; Bottlenose Dolphins.

Port Stephens is actually a drowned valley — the result of a huge rise in sea levels more than 70,000 years ago. The surrounding volcanic peaks guard a marine haven that is home to a wide range of life, both above and below the ocean.

A resident population of around 80 Bottlenose Dolphins have endeared themselves to Port Stephens locals and visiting tourists. Some of these dolphins wear distinctive scars and have been recognisable to tour operators for more than 40 years. During winter, a few thousand of the dolphin's cetaceous relatives, Humpback Whales, pass by Port Stephens on their annual breeding migration north. Since the ban on whale hunting in Australia, their numbers have steadily increased and their tail-slapping antics can be observed from elevated points on shore.

Less commonly seen is the Gould's Petrel. This extremely rare ocean bird breeds on Cabbage Tree Island, a kilometre out from the bay's entrance. It is the only known breeding site for the few hundred pairs of birds remaining in the world. Other islands around Port Stephens, such as Broughton, provide rookeries and safe nesting areas for seagulls, shearwaters, Little Penguin and Ospreys.

Nelson Bay was once occupied by the Worimi tribe, the local Aborigines of Port Stephens, and then settled by white farmers during the early 1800s. After its agricultural base was established, the town directed its economic activity towards shipping. These key local industries continued into the 1920s until the Hunter Valley was deemed better land for vineyards and wheat. Today, the area contains the popular **Hunter Region Botanic Gardens** (in Heathcote), known for its annual Spring Fair and its 140 ha of theme gardens, bushland walks, wildflowers and native vegetation. Down at the beach, **Shoal Bay's** sandy shores and clear pastel waters are home to a resident dolphin population. For swimmers there is no shortage of relaxing seascapes — **Fingal Bay**, **Anna Bay**, **Soliders Point** and **Salamander Bay** are all postcard-perfect attractions of this area.

Hunter Region Botanic Gardens

West of Sydney

Far from the ocean breezes and sea swells of Sydney's coast, the Blue Mountains lie beyond the suburban sprawl of Sydney's vast western suburbs. The grandeur of the Blue Mountains and their towering monoliths contrasts with the area's quaint villages and homes. Tourist-oriented "cottage businesses" sit side by side with country-style tea houses, rural guesthouses, art galleries and long-standing hotels. Thanks to a modern train and transport infrastructure, the Blue Mountains are readily accessible to visitors from Sydney; likewise, residents of the mountains have an easy commute to the CBD via express train services to Sydney's Central Station.

Female grey-headed flying fox and young

Nature's Splendour

The Blue Mountains and their surrounds are easily reached by visitors thanks to a well-organised tourist trade and the affiliated businesses that have grown to service the area. Several breathtaking scenic cable cars service the area, along with walking tracks and other sightseeing attractions, allowing visitors to witness firsthand the steep cliffs, forests and other natural wonders of this dramatic area.

In addition to **Blue Mountains National Park**, visitors can also journey into **Kanangra–Boyd National Park**, where walking tours cater to safe exploration of deep caves and other fascinating landmarks. The elevated lookouts in the park showcase other equally impressive natural wonders and provide an insight into the landscape and geology of this time-honoured region. A geological centrepiece of the Blue Mountains is **Jenolan Caves**, a series of deep underground chasms filled with intriguing stalactite and stalagmite formations. The other-worldly structures encountered in the caves makes for a truly memorable experience. No less remarkable are the **Three Sisters** (*right*), poised precariously on the edge of a rocky promontory. They are, perhaps, the most famous of all the Blue Mountain's many attractions. Whether your aim is some relaxed sightseeing, visits to rural townships or hard trekking over the national park's craggy plateaus, the landscape surrounding this magnificent area of Greater Sydney is a must-see for any visitor to New South Wales.

Blue of the Blue Mountains

One of the Blue Mountains (*above*) most prominent features is the enduring haze of ethereal blue that fills the air. It remains a source of vexation to the national park's many visitors, yet the answer to the "riddle of the blue" lies everywhere in the surrounding environment.

The dominant tree species in the Blue Mountains is the eucalypt: the leaves of which have an especially high oil content. The vapour from eucalypt oil hangs over the mountains and refracts the light from the sun, giving the air its characteristic blue tinge.

Eucalypt oil is extremely flammable. Gum trees, however, are well adapted to bush fires and even depend on them to germinate seeds.

Top to bottom: **The Blue Mountains; Autumn in Norman Lindsay gardens; Jenolan Caves; Pinecrest Garden, Leura.**

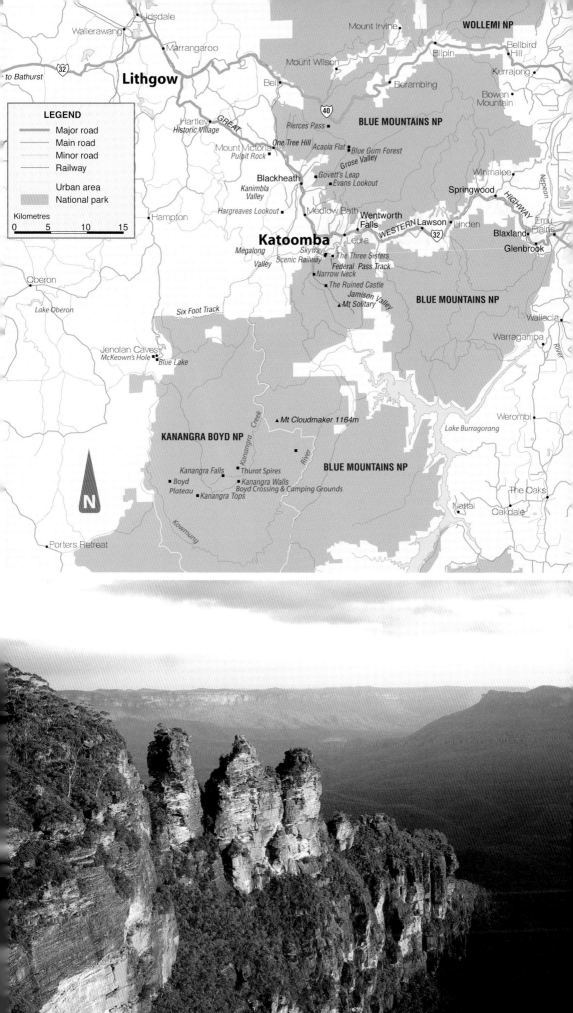

LEGEND

Major road
Main road
Minor road
Railway

Urban area
National park

Kilometres
0   5   10   15

to Bathurst
Lidsdale
Wallerawang
Marrangaroo
Lithgow
Hartley Historic Village
GREAT
Mount Victoria
Pulpit Rock
Blackheath
Kanimbla Valley
Hampton
Hargreaves Lookout
Medlow Bath
Megalong Valley
Scenic Railway
Skyway
Katoomba
Leura
Wentworth Falls
WESTERN
Lawson
Linden
Oberon
Lake Oberon
Six Foot Track
The Three Sisters
Federal Pass Track
Narrow Neck
The Ruined Castle
Jamison Valley
Mt Solitary
Jenolan Caves
McKeown's Hole
Blue Lake

Mount Irvine
WOLLEMI NP
Bilpin
Bellbird Hill
Kurrajong
Mount Wilson
Berambing
Bowen Mountain
Bell
Pierces Pass
One Tree Hill
Acacia Flat
Blue Gum Forest
Grose Valley
Govett's Leap
Evans Lookout
BLUE MOUNTAINS NP
Winmalee
Springwood
HIGHWAY
Nepean River
Emu Plains
Blaxland
Glenbrook
BLUE MOUNTAINS NP
Wallacia
Warragamba
River
Weronbi
Lake Burragorang
Mt Cloudmaker 1164m
Kanangra Creek
River
KANANGRA BOYD NP
Kanangra Falls
Thurat Spires
Boyd Plateau
Kanangra Walls
Boyd Crossing & Camping Grounds
Kanangra Tops
Kowmung
BLUE MOUNTAINS NP
The Oaks
Nattai
Oakdale
Porters Retreat

N

Blue Mountains

The blue-tinged **Blue Mountains**, 100 km west of Sydney, and the ancient rock formations of the area, such as the **Three Sisters**, **Ruined Castle** and **Pulpit Rock**, attract local and international visitors, year-round. The rugged, high-altitude region was for a long time considered impenetrable, until a successful crossing by explorers Gregory Blaxland, William Wentworth and William Lawson in 1813.

Blaxland, Lawson and Wentworth hacked through dense bush for 18 days in the hope of either finding or forcing a path through the mountains. With the crossing completed, the mountains were opened up to visitors and the construction of stately country homes soon followed. A road was cut in 1814 by William Cox and a team of 30 convicts and, in a little over three months, they had cut 50 miles of roadway to **Mount York**. Within six months they had cut a further 50 miles of road to **Bathurst**, a major centre for agriculture and, within 20 years, tourism in the area had really begun to flourish.

Today the Blue Mountains — part of the **Great Dividing Range** stretching from Gippsland, Victoria, to the rainforests of northern Queensland — is one of Greater Sydney's most beloved rural retreats. The many miles of untouched wilderness, crisp, clean air and mountainous scenery make it a favourite with both Australian and international visitors. The region is centred around **Katoomba**, the largest town in the Blue Mountains, which is home to the region's main train station and the **Three Sisters**. **Echo Point**, 2 km from the town centre and featuring awe-inspiring panoramas, is the best vantage for observing this incredible sandstone marvel.

Leura Falls promises quiet respite from the hectic pace of city living.

King's Tablelands To stand anywhere along this remarkable curving rim is to be on the true brink of wilderness.

Echo Point also has good views of other Blue Mountains landmarks such as **Jamison Valley**, **Narrow Neck**, **Falls Reserve** and **Mount Solitary**, along with walking track departure points. A well-equipped and informative visitor centre is also located here.

Katoomba

Early industry in Katoomba blossomed with the opening of the **Katoomba Coal Mine**, which has given the region one of its trademark attractions: a cable car track cut into the cliff to transport coal from the valley floor. It is now utilised by the **Scenic Railway** to take passengers along the steepest railway in the world, travelling some 400 m down to the base of the Jamison Valley. Alternatively, anyone with enough energy can traverse the 800 steps of the **Giant Stairway**. Close to the Scenic Railway is the **Scenic Skyway**, an elevated box-car travelling half a kilometre across the Jamison Valley. It provides a much different perspective from the traditional land-based vantages and lookouts.

Blackheath

Blackheath is the highest township in the Blue Mountains, elevated 1000 m above sea level. Its pure air and fertile landscape facilitate the growth of superb rhododendron gardens, the basis for an annual show each November.

Views of Katoomba A town blessed with a glorious backyard.

Three Sister's Lookout at Echo Point.

Mount Victoria

Mount Victoria is the most westerly of the Blue Mountains townships. This historic small village, originally named **One Tree Hill**, contains a large number of heritage buildings. Several other attractive townships are also scattered throughout the mountains, including **Leura**, perhaps the prettiest of the region's villages. Two kilometres beyond is the grandeur of **Wentworth Falls**, named after William Wentworth. Stunning views centred on the immense Wentworth Falls waterfall are best experienced from the walking tracks through the **Valley of the Waters**.

Scenic World

The Scenic Railway (*top right*), the steepest incline railway in the world, provides a 415 m descent through the surrounding rainforest to the start of the Scenic Walkway — an informative 2 km boardwalk that links up with the Scenic Flyway (*below*) or Scenic Skyway (*bottom right*). The latter takes its passengers on a 720 m "flight" over the Jamison Valley. The cable car has a glass-bottom floor for real heart-in-the-mouth views of the ravines and waterfalls below.

Further Information

1 **Echo Point Visitor Information Centre**
   Echo Point Road, Katoomba
   (Ph: 02 4739 6266)

2 **Glenbrook Visitor Information Centre**
   Great Western Highway, Glenbrook
   (Ph: 1300 653 408)

3 **National Parks and Wildlife Heritage Centre**
   Govetts Leap Road, Blackheath
   (Ph: 02 4787 8877)

Top to bottom: **The Katoomba Court House** was opened in 1896 and declared to be "one of the most comfortable and elegant in the colony"; **Hydro Majestic** The most famous icon in Medlow Bath.

Leura

Leura's carefully manicured gardens and streets have made the township a popular destination. It holds a garden festival every October. The cooler climate suits many varieties of flowers and shrubs that will not grow around Sydney. Visit the **Leura Visitor Centre** (Shop 4, 208, The Mall, Ph: 02 4784 2222).

Left to right: **Blackheath Glen; Bacchante Gardens; Grose Valley** All perfect displays of nature and its varied splendour.

The Three Sisters are the focal point of the Blue Mountains.

Blue Mountains National Park

The rugged Blue Mountains have both a rich Indigenous and European heritage. The vastness of the national park spoils its visitors for different choices of recreation. Each weekend teams of sightseers arrive in the mountains to sample the sights, sounds and solitude of the area, bringing a total of over three million visitors per year to the Blue Mountains.

The park has recently joined other international icons on the World Heritage List and became one of more than a dozen Australian-listed sites. A daytrip from Sydney is not nearly long enough to fully experience this wilderness. Key attractions of the region can be seen in a day, but longer time frames are needed for a full appreciation of the mountains.

The Three Sisters

In common with many Aboriginal legends, these rock formations are said to mark the spot of the metamorphosed bodies of Dreamtime beings. One legend has it that long ago a clever old man called Tyawan lived in the mountains. He had three daughters — Meenhi, Wimlah and Gunnedoo — and a magic shinbone that changed him into a lyrebird when he wished.

The Three Sisters, overlooking Jamison Valley to Ruined Castle.

When Tyawan went hunting he would warn his daughters to stay on the cliff, safe from Bunyip — a fearsome beast who lived deep in the valley.

One day Meenhi knocked a rock over the cliff; it crashed into the valley, waking Bunyip, who charged up the cliff toward the terrified girls. Tyawan could not reach them in time and so he changed them into rocks. Enraged, Bunyip chased Tyawan, who made his escape by changing into a lyrebird. But Tyawan dropped his magic shinbone when his arms transformed into wings. Ever since, the lyrebird has scratched in the leaves, looking for the shinbone that will release his daughters from their stone prison.

Bushwalking

Bushwalking is big in the mountains. Dramatic seasonal changes, in both the landscape and foliage, and a wealth of unique flora and fauna, make this a popular pastime any month of the year. Some of the Blue Mountains bushwalks take up to one week to complete. The weather fluctuates through greater extremes — when compared with central Sydney, some 100 km to the east — and trekkers should be prepared for rapid changes in temperature and conditions.

From the various elevated vantage points on the cliffs and ledges of the national park, you'll see hazy blue valleys and mountain ranges merge with distant hilltops, rocky outcrops, cascading waterfalls, quiet rivers, mist-shrouded ravines and dense rainforest.

Blue Mountains National Park contains many excellent campsites, most of which are close to major attractions. A topographic map and compass are necessary for serious hikes but one of the park's grandest walks — the 5 km **Grand Canyon Track** — only requires casual wear, a bottle of water and a pair of comfortable shoes.

Mermaid's Cave

Blue Mountains Walks

1 **Princes Rock Walk** (1 km, ½ hr, easy)

2 **Weeping Rock–Fletchers Lookout Track** (1 km, 1 hr, medium-hard)

3 **Govetts Leap Descent** (1.3 km, 1.5 hr, hard)

4 **Glenbrook Gorge Track** (1.5 km, 3 hr, hard)

5 **Mount Banks Track** (1.5 km, 1.5 hr, medium-hard)

The journey culminates in wide sweeping views across **Grose Valley**. From Echo Point, site of the **Katoomba Visitors Centre** and the Three Sisters lookout, is the departure point of another equally enjoyable walk: the **Federal Pass Track.** At a little over 5 km, it is a lengthy trek that takes in many of the Blue Mountains' scenic highlights.

The track weaves its way through some truly majestic wilderness, incorporating immense stone staircases and spectacular streams, waterfalls, rainforests and elevated lookouts. A three-hour round trip returns visitors to Echo Point.

From **Govetts Leap Lookout** at Blackheath, the **Pulpit Rock Track** leads trampers on a 6 km adventure to the imposing landmark of **Pulpit Rock** — a lone pinnacle, standing high against the awesome backdrop of Grose Valley.

The dense outcrop of tall trees at **Blue Gum Forest** can be reached after a moderately strenuous, 8 km trek from **Pierces Pass.** The walk passes through a landscape of lush native rainforest and flowing creeks. **Fairy Grotto Rainforest** gives way to tall trees leading down to the **Grose River** crossing point. From here there is an easy passage to Blue Gum Forest and the campgrounds of **Acacia Flat.** These are just a sample of the many fine walks around the Blackheath area.

Top to bottom: **Blue Gum Forest; Grand Canyon** — both disarmingly beautiful.

Grose Valley One of the many valleys in the region.

Committed bushwalkers and the brave can also tackle the immense **Six Foot Track**, a three-day, 42 km trek from Katoomba to Jenolan Caves by way of the original horse track (dating back to the 1880s) used for the journey between the two sites.

But There's More!

The Blue Mountains region is also known as the "City of the Arts" and regular cultural and creative expositions complement the spectacular natural landscape. The crisp months of winter herald the most noted occasions on the art calendar, including **Yulefest** celebrations with their colourful, Christmas-oriented cheer. The Blue Mountains' rural towns and retreats are perfectly suited to such "olde worlde" festivity — the antique dealers, galleries and historic buildings all pitch in to create an authentically charming ambience of times gone by. Accommodation is available in properties ranging from mountain resorts to cosy B&Bs, motels, backpacker hostels and cottage cabins (ideal for longer stays to soak up the magical atmosphere). The Blue Mountains and the townships' attractions are best accessed by public transport from Sydney via train services from Central Station. Call CountryLink (Ph: 13 2232) or contact the Blue Mountains National Park and the Echo Point Visitor Centre for information on guided tours.

Anvil Rock Another unique sandstone feature shaped by the hand of nature.

Walking in the Blue Mountains: Don't Forget!

1   Take enough food and water for emergencies.

2   Wear comfortable footwear and protective clothing for all weather conditions.

3   Do not walk alone, always keep your party together and leave an itinerary with park rangers or with friends.

4   Take complete first aid equipment.

Honeymoon Lookout has great views of the Jamison Valley and cliff walls.

Flora and Fauna in the Blue Mountains

The unique geological evolution of the Blue Mountains, which has occurred over 300 million years, has gifted the area with a range of botanical habitats that, in turn, support a great variety of animals. The Blue Mountains comprise open eucalypt forests (grassy, sparsely-treed areas that dominate the region's ridges and upper valleys), closed forests (trees that are more closely packed together in the cooler, low-lying gullies and slopes), wet and dry heathlands (characterised by short shrubs and stumpy trees on mountain plateaus), rainforests (areas of densely packed vegetation in sheltered gorges and deep ravines), and swamps (in waterlogged areas with poor drainage). The Blue Mountains are teeming with wildlife. Over 400 different animal species are attracted to these habitats and there are a handful of threatened species that survive here, including the Spotted-tailed Quoll, the Long-nosed Potoroo, the Blue Mountains Water Skink, and the Green and Golden Bell Frog.

Mammals

Eastern Pygmy-possum

Mammals are abundant across most environments of the Blue Mountains, but it takes patience and a keen pair of eyes to observe them in their natural state. This is due to the fact that many of these mammals are nocturnal. Many species of possums and gliders, as well as bats, bandicoots and carnivorous marsupials such as the antechinus and quoll, prefer to forage or hunt for food under the cover of darkness. Antechinus species particularly like bogs, where snails, worms and other tasty invertebrate treats are in abundance.

In the open forests, Short-beaked Echidnas expose termites by digging into the ground and tearing apart rotten logs or mounds with their powerful claws. They are easily disturbed and, once they have burrowed into the ground, are well-camouflaged. Koalas are immobile, furry lumps for the best part of 20 hours a day and it is hard to spot them high in the treetops of the open forests.

Brushtail Possums favour rainforest environments where fruits and seeds are plentiful, and where movement between trees is easily achieved. The Bush Rat roams the moist rainforest floor where it can forage for fungi and other plant material. Another inhabitant of densely forested gullies is the Grey-headed Flying Fox, which gathers in large, squabbling colonies and enjoys the rich smorgasbord of fruits that the rainforest serves.

The swamps of the Blue Mountains support ferns and sedges which the Swamp Wallaby relishes as food. This wallaby is more diurnal than most other macropods and may be observed by cautious visitors. Red-necked Wallabies can be found bounding through stands of eucalypts and Red-legged Pademelons (*top left*) inhabit the outer fringes.

Mountain Brushtail Possum

Red-necked Wallaby

Sugar Glider

Reptiles and Amphibians

Snakes are common in the Blue Mountains and a number of venomous and non-venomous species enjoy a (mostly) secretive life here. Eastern Blind Snakes (burrowing, worm-like snakes that are extremely sensitive to light and feed on termites and ants) live in the loose soil of open forests. Death adders use the cover of leaf litter within closed forests to ambush their prey. Wriggling the slim tip of their fat tails, they lure unsuspecting rodents into a deadly trap. The large but harmless Diamond Python is another regularly seen resident.

Lizards, such as the Blue Mountains Water Skink, can be found basking on grassy tussocks in the heaths near Leura, Wentworth Falls and Newnes Plateau. Water Dragons and Long-Necked Tortoises dwell around and within the rivers and waterways. Frogs, too, thrive in these rainforest environments. The Bleating Tree-frog is just one of the many frog species that can be heard in symphony with the rush of fresh, mountain water of the region.

Bleating Tree-frog

Diamond Python

Birds and Birdwatching

The Blue Mountains are a real paradise for both native birds and
birdwatchers alike. The many types of mountain habitats appeal to a huge
range of bird species, and a day spent in any of these environments will
prove to be a rewarding visual and auditory experience for any birdwatcher.

The open eucalypt forests attract the most boisterous and jovial
characters in the great circus of Australian birds. High up in the branches,
Laughing Kookaburras can be heard spreading cheer throughout the
bush, competing with raucous flocks of colourful cockatoos, including the
Sulphur-crested and Gang Gang Cockatoo, which screech and shriek beside
trees full of trilling Rosellas. In the understorey, flowering banksias and
grevilleas tempt honeyeaters, silvereyes and other nectar aficionados like
the Eastern Spinebill. Listen out for the ringing ventriloquism of the Crested
Bellbird, and keep an eye out for some of the more diminutive species, such
as the Scarlet Robin and Red-browed Finch.

Red-browed Finch

In the closed forests, the Pilotbird scratches in the leaf litter for insects,
spiders and other invertebrates. The Superb Lyrebird, another resident of
the dense forest, is the undisputed master of mimicry, imitating perfectly,
the calls of other birds, camera shutters and ringtones from mobile phones.

The rainforests are home to the Eastern Whipbird, rarely seen but easily
recognised by the swishing crack of its call. Another curious denizen of this
area is the Satin Bowerbird: connoisseur of blue trinkets, which it uses to
embellish its elaborate bower in the hope of attracting female mates.

Scarlet Robin

Left to right: Yellow-tailed Black Cockatoo; Sulphur-crested Cockatoo; Gang-Gang Cockatoo;
Crimson Rosella; Eastern Rosella; Australian King-Parrot.

Flora

Open forests are the most common habitat in the Blue Mountains and the
most prominent species of this environment is the eucalyptus. The types of
gum trees are many and varied and include Black Ash, Red Bloodwood, she-
oaks, stringy-barks, scribbly gums and Sydney Red Gums. Flowering plants,
such as wattles and hakeas, are prevalent and it is worth keeping an eye out
for the distinctive Mountain Devil and New South Wales' floral emblem,
the Waratah.

The magnificent Blue Gum is the botanical flagship of the cool, closed
forests. Blue Gum Forest is an outstanding site for observing its namesake.
The forest can be accessed from Grose Valley from either Perrys Lookdown
or Pierces Pass. The moist forest floor is alive with other vegetation. Various
mosses and fungi grow here, as does the gigantic King Fern. Beautiful
flowers, boronias and orchids, can also be appreciated in the closed forests.

A veritable kaleidoscope of flowers explode over the heathlands
during spring. Pea flowers, flannel flowers, conesticks, and guinea flowers
cast a vibrant blanket over these open areas. There are some excellent
tracks around the Blue Mountains that allow visitors to view this natural
phenomenon — the Rocket Point Lookout Track, Pulpit Rock Track, and Cliff
Top Track all provide great access to the mountain's dry heathlands.

Blue Gum Forest

Myrtle

Mountain Devil

Boronia, a member of the citrus family.

Kanangra–Boyd National Park

Boyd Plateau

Boyd Plateau is an immense dome of elevated land that abruptly gives way to dramatic cliffs, waterfalls and valleys. Wildlife spotters are frequently rewarded at Boyd Crossing. The variety of fauna is complemented by the area's massive wilderness of deep gorges, ravines, rivers and lookout points.

The dramatic grandeur of Blue Mountains National Park continues into **Kanangra–Boyd National Park** to the south-west. The park, two hours drive from Sydney, forms part of the rugged Blue Mountains World Heritage Area. Its distance from Sydney makes it quite a journey for the more time-conscious traveller but, nonetheless, many tourists undertake the pilgrimage to Kanangra–Boyd's most famous attraction — the astonishing **Jenolan Caves**.

Wildlife, camping and bushwalking treks are available. Some 4WD roads cut through the park, but most sightseeing is undertaken through the least trafficked sections of the park.

Kanangra–Boyd National Park lies to the south and west of the Blue Mountains.

Some of these tracks are only available to properly prepared, experienced bushwalkers. This somewhat rugged and inaccessible aspect of Kanangra–Boyd is what gives the park its edge over more "tame" national parks.

Kanangra–Boyd's dramatic scenery and untouched wilds mark it as a popular spot for extreme sports and adventure activities, such as rock climbing and abseiling. For less strenuous, but equally enjoyable, activities, **Kanangra Walls** is the preferred attraction. Some of the park's best lookouts are readily accessible via brief walks from this magnificent area, with its attractive waterfall and abseiling spots. These include **Plateau Walk**, a longer hike onto the pretty, heath-covered plateau of **Kanangra Tops**. The most popular walk is the **Lookout Walk**, taking in extensive views of **Kanangra Creek**, **Mount Cloudmaker** and the distant Blue Mountains.

Remarkable Caves

In this area noted for its alluring geology, perhaps the most distinctive natural phenomena can be found at the **Jenolan Caves** — a subterranean fantasy land of deep limestone caverns. There are over 20 major caves in the system and nine of them are open for guided tours. The **Jenolan Caves Reserve Trust** (Ph: 02 6359 3911) provides in-depth visitor information.

The popular **Lucas Cave** has a lengthy guided tour, while **Imperial Cave** is convenient for brief exploration. **Chifley Cave** (named after 1950s Prime Minister Ben Chifley) is another popular option, noted for its moody, coloured lighting.

The nine main caves are spread across two caverns in the interior of a huge natural archway. Known to local Aboriginals in the area, (they had named the caves *Binoomea* or "dark places"), the caves were first discovered by the 19th-century bushranger, cattle thief and escaped convict, James McKeown, who routinely passed through the large, shadowy arch en route to his secluded hideaway on the far side of Jenolan Caves.

Attempts to trace and capture the elusive McKeown exposed the majesty of the caves to the public. The main road to the caves still cuts through this gloomy archway today, bursting out into bright daylight on its far side.

The two sides of the arch were named the **Devils Coach House** (south of the arch) and the **Grand Archway** (to the north). The "Devils Coach House" was the initial description given by McKeown's arch-pursuer, James Whalan, when tailing McKeown through the darkened archway. McKeown was eventually captured, his hideaway being a hole in the rocky mountain side now known as McKeown's Hole.

Multi-cave tour tickets are available for dedicated cavers. The Lucas Cave and **Orient Cave** tour is a popular double-header. This tour explores the vast chambers in Lucas Cave and the crystalline decorations of Orient Cave. **Chifley, Imperial** and **Jubilee Caves** are situated in the southern arch of the Devils Coach House, while the other caves are to the north in the Grand Archway.

Overall, Jenolan Caves impart a truly magical, glittering mystique. Many sections of the limestone formations are floodlit for enhanced viewing. The remarkable and fantastic "speleothem" (cave formations) found here include columns, stalagmites, stalactites and calcite pool crystals. Orient Cave features an array of particularly garish speleothems, coloured in attractive shades of red, brown and yellow, as well as glowing white formations.

Other highlights of Jenolan Caves include the **Crystal Cities** and **Fluted Column** of Imperial Cave, and the **River Cave's Grand Column and Minaret,** as well as the **Angel's Wings** in the **Temple of Baal** cave.

The Jenolan region surrounding the caves is some 2500 ha of bushland that teems with readily observed wildlife, including kangaroos and lyrebirds. Notable landmarks, both natural and artificial, include the long-standing guesthouse of **Jenolan Caves Resort,** built in 1898, **Blue Lake** and the attractions of nearby towns such as **Lithgow** and **Hartley Historic Village.**

The Toll Keeper's Cottage, Mount Victoria Built in 1849 it is a reminder of times when travellers had to pay a toll.

Imperial Hotel, Mount Victoria Impressive accommodation built in 1878.

Mt Wilson rainforest Many plants flourish in the cooler climate.

Caves House, Jenolan Caves is a distinguished place to lodge while exploring the area.

Jenolan Caves showing a minaret stalactite formation built by slow deposits of calcite.

Zig Zag Railway One of Lithgow's more famous routes once enabled trains to transport coal.

South of Sydney

As Sydney's vibrant southern suburbs give way to the lush vegetation of Royal National Park, the park also gives way to the industry and suburbia of coastal Wollongong. Along this stretch of coast lie perennially popular towns noted for their attractiveness and the

Waratah

numerous outdoor activities they offer. Inland, the landscape is shaped by agriculture, rustic charm and the rolling slopes of the Southern Highlands. Nattai and Thirlmere Lakes National Parks give visitors to this region the best of both worlds — a chance to experience the scenic coast and its surrounding rural climes.

Much to See and Do

Further south from **Wollongong**, the **Illawarra** and **Shoalhaven** regions display a rich vista of fascinating natural landmarks — long, secluded beaches and unspoilt national parks. Wollongong is the main urban centre of Illawarra and welcomes visitors with its appealing blend of traditional and contemporary lifestyles. Surrounded by mountains and sea, and centred on an attractive circular harbour, it is a picturesque town with a relaxed pace and many attractions. **Port Kembla** is the major shipping port to its south. To its north are a series of much-loved beaches stretching all the way from Wollongong to **Royal National Park**.

Also south of Sydney lies the grand **Southern Highlands** region, a fertile area of farming, produce and cosy country towns. The suitably energetic visitor can explore the region on foot, undertaking the lengthy seven-day walk from **Katoomba** in the Blue Mountains region, known as the **Barallier Track**.

Attractive nearby towns include **Bowral** and **Mittagong.** Bowral hosts an annual tulip festival, **Tulip Time**, a popular family-oriented event that attracts flower lovers from far and wide. There are many areas to Sydney's south that proudly portray the distinct beauty of this part of Australia. **Fitzroy Falls** in the Southern Highlands and **Morton National Park** are just two of the great attractions in this celebrated region.

Other national parks in these parts include **Nattai** and **Thirlmere Lakes.** For the adventurous, a different kind of view can be experienced from the nature reserve at **Stanwell Park.** This is the home of **Bald Hill**, a hang-gliding haven well served by experienced tour operators.

Southern Highlands

Quaint English villages meet classic Scottish landscapes in Australia's high country: a nostaglic amalgam of European charm and local history.

A scattering of small, pretty towns nestled throughout the Highlands, each with their own unique character and attractions, holds special appeal for visitors.

Each spring, Bowral hosts one of the country's most famous floral festivals — Tulip Time. Corbett Gardens (*bottom right*) is the horticultural heartbeat of the town and blooms with colour during the festival.

Tradition is also rich in Kangaroo Valley, where Hampden Bridge, spanning the idyllic Kangaroo River, is a stately relic of colonial times. Opened in 1898, this handsome castellated bridge is the oldest suspension bridge in Australia.

Top to bottom: **Wollongong Harbour; Kiama; Jervis Bay; Murramarang National Park.**

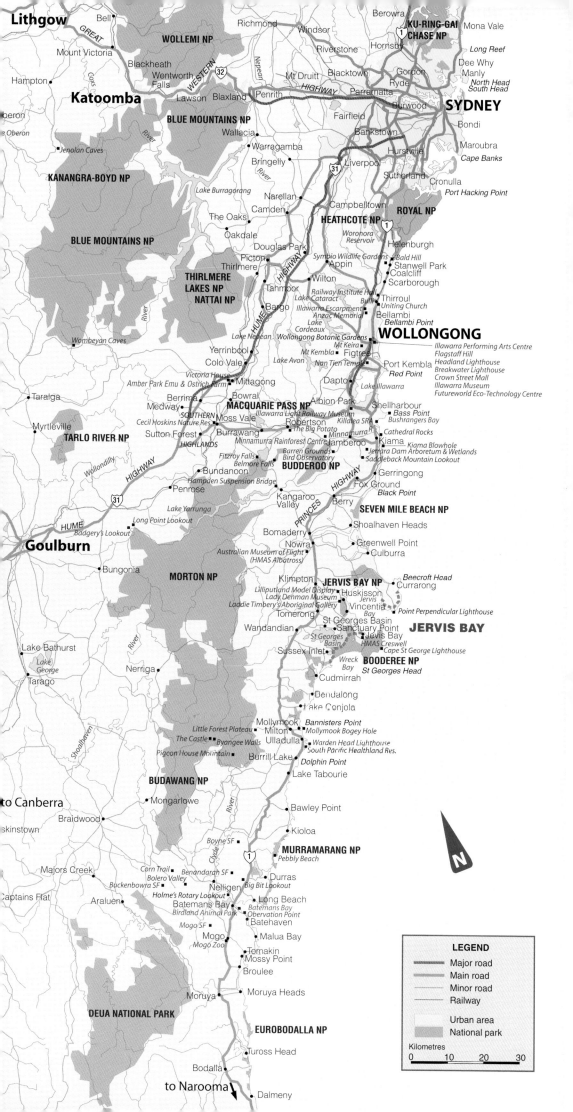

Southern Highlands

The seven-day journey along the **Barallier Track**, from Katoomba, leads visitors into the New South Wales **Southern Highlands**. Qualifying as one of the State's best long walks, it gives walkers an in-depth study of the nature of this inspiring region.

Upon arrival in the Southern Highlands, committed bushwalkers and trekkers can take in the **Boxvale Mine Walking Track**. The **Wombeyan Caves** are also near the township of **Mittagong**, giving hikers the chance to investigate caves as beautiful and intriguing as the more famous Jenolan Caves of Blue Mountains National Park.

With four distinct seasons, the inland climate of the Southern Highlands is more variable than the coastal weather experienced in Sydney's city centre. The region has built its name around its relaxed pace, fertile farming and cattle lands, manicured gardens and friendly rural ways.

The **Southern Highlands Visitor Information Centre** (62–70 Main Street, Mittagong, Ph: 02 4871 2888) provides information on all Southern Highlands attractions, including the noted **Amber Park Emu and Ostrich Farm**, where tours introduce visitors to huge flightless birds such as the Emu, Ostrich, Southern Cassowary and the South American Rhea.

Mittagong The town's streets, which are lined with humble homes and shops, are designed for quiet meandering.

Wombeyan Caves

About 65 km west of Mittagong in the Burragorang Valley is the intriguing natural oddity of Wombeyan Caves. Five separate cave tours, including the Fig Tree Cave (*left*) allow visitors to experience a fantastic underworld of strangely sculptured limestone. There are also overnight cottages, camping and caravan facilities. The caves are open daily from 8.30 a.m. – 4 p.m.

Crafty Creations

Mittagong has gained a reputation for its arts and crafts and deservedly so. Its cottage industry produces charming collectibles (such as vintage-style dolls) and has a strong emphasis on needlework. A visit to the needlework homestead of **Victoria House** (on the Hume Highway at Mittagong, Ph: 02 4871 1682) is well worth the effort for its stunning selection of tapestry, embroidery and vintage dolls. **Moss Vale** is another important town within the region and is widely considered to be the antique capital of an area famous for its range of collectibles.

Visitors from Old Blimey will instantly feel at home here. The whole area is reminiscent of a classic English village, with its quaint atmosphere and country charm. The **Moss Vale Visitors Centre and Historic Walk** is a good introduction to the town's attractions. With a discovery guide in hand, visitors can view the many stately country homes and prosperous farms that dot the surrounding landscape.

Bundanoon A pretty and quiet town, Bundanoon was a favourite spot for honeymooners in the 1940s, continuing to attract many visitors today.

The Old Bakery Cottage at Berrima.

Outside these towns lie rugged wilderness areas, such as **Budawang National Park** and **Morton National Park** (home of the spectacular **Fitzroy Falls**). This waterfall is easily accessible and there are some excellent walks and lookouts in the area. Its namesake, the small township of Fitzroy Falls, lies on the main road between **Kangaroo Valley** and the South Coast town of **Nowra**. The **Cecil Hoskins Nature Reserve** (in Moss Vale) has an attractive landscape of tranquil wetlands for keen birdwatchers.

The **Cockatoo Run** steam train provides a pleasant ride from Moss Vale to **Robertson** (operating Saturday to Tuesday, Ph: 1800 64 3801), bringing passengers to the premier potato growing region of New South Wales, resplendent with its obligatory "Big Potato" landmark.

Cricket Highlight

Bowral is another Southern Highland town with interesting cultural detours. While there, sports fans will be treated to some important cricketing history, thanks to the town's most famous export, batting legend Sir Donald Bradman. The **Bradman Museum** (St Jude St, Bowral, Ph: 02 4862 1247) emphasises the conservation of cricketing heritage and promotes the future development of the sport.

Natural History: Thirlmere Lakes NP

One of the last undisturbed lake systems in the greater Sydney region, Thirlmere Lakes National Park is an unique wetland area of significant ecological value.

Comprised of five rush-fringed lakes (*right*), Thirlmere is over two million years old and has sustained the evolution of a number of rare species (including a type of freshwater sponge and jellyfish). The lakes also home to Australian Wood Ducks (*below*).

Bradman Museum, Bowral

Bowral

Bowral's "olde-worlde" charm is an echo from the nation's past; the town is a popular place for antique shopping, collectibles and other rural handicrafts. A jaunt into the neighbouring village of **Berrima** is a pleasant side trip for visitors seeking out the essence of authentic Georgian towns from Australia's colonial times.

Close by, the significant **Nattai National Park**, enclosing the immense **Lake Burragorang**, and **Thirlmere Lakes National Park**, with its five freshwater lakes and abundance of birdlife, can be easily accessed. Nattai was declared a national park in 1991 to protect its landscape and geological features. It is part of the **Greater Blue Mountains World Heritage Area** and home to **Warragamba Dam**, which supplies 80% of Sydney's water.

Fitzroy Falls The falls plunge over 81 m down the sandstone cliffs into the Yarrunga Valley.

Leighton Gardens, Moss Vale are in the centre of town and have massed displays of flowers in spring and autumn. A smaller version of the famous gardens can be found in Bowral.

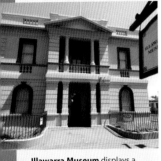

Illawarra Museum displays a collection of memorabilia from the city's pioneering days.

Harbourfront Restaurant, Belmore Basin has pleasant views and tasty cuisine.

North Wollongong is typical of the beaches in this region.

Flagstaff Hill invites quiet contemplation.

Wollongong

Wollongong is a major city an hour south of Sydney's city centre and 45 minutes from the Southern Highlands. Centred on an attractive harbour, the city is a blend of residential suburbia, shipping, shopping, industry, education and heritage.

Mount Keira is an ideal vantage point for surveying the area — its elevated position permitting panoramic views and scenic walks of the surrounding lands. Conveniently distanced from Sydney, Wollongong has developed its own character while retaining transport routes to the CBD (via rail and also by road along the Princes Highway leading directly north) for workers employed in Sydney.

Wollongong is situated right in the heartland of the South Coast and Illawarra region and provides urban, country and coastal living. With the vast expanse of Pacific Ocean cobalt to its east, and the grandeur of the **Illawarra Mountains** to the west, it is cradled in an area of spectacular beauty. Lacking the bustling, hyper-energy of Sydney's crowded throngs, Wollongong maintains a pace balanced somewhere between industrious and idle, making it an attractive daytrip for visitors. The busy docklands of **Port Kembla** are directly south of Wollongong's shores and keep the heavy industry of the port a pleasant distance from Wollongong itself.

Wollongong Harbour is a tightly enclosed, circular harbour with two long stretches of beach heading directly north and south from the harbour heads. They are **North Wollongong Beach** and **Wollongong City Beach**, respectively.

Lovely Lighthouses

Wollongong is the only point on the east coast of Australia that has two lighthouses, and they are in close proximity to each other. The city also has a substantial fishing fleet and maritime heritage. The **Wollongong Headland Lighthouse**, situated on the windswept headland area of Flagstaff Hill, sits beside artillery that fortified Wollongong Harbour in the 19th century. The parkland surrounding the Wollongong Headland Lighthouse is a popular picnic and sightseeing area with a guided heritage walk offering glimpses into the history of the ever-popular harbour.

At the harbour's northern end stands the smaller **Wollongong Breakwater Lighthouse**.

Glorious Gardens

Perhaps the region's most notable manicured landscape is that found in the **Wollongong Botanic Gardens** (61 Northfields Avenue, Keiraville, Ph: 02 4225 2636). Established in 1970, the garden features rainforest areas, an extensive rose garden, succulent gardens, and the **Sir Joseph Banks Plant House** with its collection of plants from the sultry Australian tropics, deserts and temperate regions. Further afield is the delightful **Symbio Wildlife Gardens** (7–11 Lawrence Hargrave Drive, Stanwell Tops, Ph: 02 4294 1244), which is a large zoo set amid 16 acres of bushland.

Japanese Garden, Wollongong Botanic Gardens One of the many garden delights.

Wollongong Botanic Gardens were transformed from paddocks in 1970.

The Conservatorium of Music, Botanic Gardens, Wollongong, is housed in the historic Gleniffer Brae Manor House.

Left to right: Wollongong Headland Lighthouse; Wollongong Harbour with Wollongong Breakwater Lighthouse.

Nan Tien Temple

Nan Tien, translated from Chinese, literally means "Paradise of the South". The Nan Tien Temple (Ph: 02 4272 0600) in the Wollongong suburb of Berkeley is the Southern Hemisphere's largest Buddhist temple. Since opening in 1995, Nan Tien has attracted many thousands of local and international visitors. The architecture, lighting and decoration of the temple are extremely beautiful and it has received a number of design awards. The surrounding gardens are particularly photogenic. This tranquil place is one of Wollongong's must-see attractions.

The many animals that visitors can observe at Symbio Wildlife Gardens include Koalas, wallaroos, Red Kangaroos, Swamp Wallabies, Emus, Echidnas, wombats, Dingos, snakes, turtles and lizards.

Attractions in and around the Region

The **Illawarra Performing Arts Centre** or IPAC, (32 Burelli Street, Wollongong, Ph: 02 4226 3366) is the region's most revered performing arts venue. For history buffs, the **Illawarra Museum** (11 Market Square, Wollongong, Ph: 02 4228 7770) provides detailed insights into the early days of Wollongong's European history. Other displays of the region's history can be found at the **Black Diamond District Heritage Centre.**

Situated in the **Bulli Heritage Centre** (Park Road, Bulli Railway Station, Ph: 02 4267 4312), this volunteer-operated museum formed in 1989 at the old Bulli Railway Station. "Black Diamond" was the term used to describe coal during Bulli's early settlement, the rock bringing great prosperity to the Illawarra region. The museum now houses a fully restored signal box room, old railway equipment and other local memorabilia including a fascinating display housed in the station's former waiting room.

More contemporary displays are found at **Futureworld Eco-Technology Centre** (1A Bridge Street, Coniston, Ph: 02 4226 9147). The interactive displays aim to improve awareness of eco-technologies that can be used for protecting the Earth's natural resources. Exhibits include intriguing South Coast inventions the prototype Solar Sailor (the solar ferry that now runs on Sydney Harbour) and the solar car that travelled from Darwin to Adelaide.

Merry Markets

For eager shoppers, **Crown Street Mall** (in the heart of the city) offers plenty of retail therapy and a number of eateries that help recharge the batteries of weary shoppers. Wollongong also hosts several popular markets each month, including the **Wollongong Showground Market** on Thursdays and Saturdays and the **Dapto Markets**, which are held every Sunday at the Dapto Showground. The **Austinmer Village Fair** is held on the second Sunday of every month and there is also the **Makers Market**, held every fourth Saturday in Civic Plaza. Another popular market, also in the town centre, is held every Friday on Crown Street Mall. The **Gipps Street Markets** (98 Gipps Street, Ph: 02 4295 4237) are undercover markets selling goods ranging from electrical products to bric-a-brac.

Around Wollongong

Wollongong is girded by natural features in every direction. **Mount Keira** and **Mount Kembla** are the best positions for viewing the region's coastal seascapes. To the north are **Corrimal**, **Thirroul** and **Bulli**. To the south, beyond **Port Kembla**, lies **Shellharbour** and the massive stretch of serene water at **Lake Illawarra**.

Inland is the **Illawarra Escarpment,** stretching from **Bulli Pass** in the north to **Bong Bong Pass** in the south, providing an attractive backdrop to Wollongong's modern skyline. The escarpment teems with flora and fauna and the many walking tracks that intersect the area give visitors a chance to investigate, up close, the botanical details of this magnificent habitat.

Directly inland from Lake Illawarra is **Macquarie Pass National Park**, part of the Illawarra Escarpment. The park has numerous picnic facilities and it is noted for its series of bushwalking tracks.

The area was declared a national park in 1970 and serves to protect the region's collection of eucalypt forests and rainforest. The pass (part of the Illawarra Highway) is bisected by the highway and is a major route into the Illawarra coastal plain.

Macquarie Pass The surrounding national park includes large areas of rainforest.

Sea Cliff Bridge This famous coastal route, connecting Sydney and Wollongong, gives tourists and commuters a spectacular view of the seaside cliffs of the Illawarra Escarpment.

Stanwell Park

Stanwell Park, an hour south of Sydney, is one of the highlights of the South Coast and a popular destination for leisure and recreation. **Bald Hill** has long been one of Australia's favourite spots for hang-gliding and **Cliff Road** is heralded as one of the world's most impressive stretches of scenic coastline. The endless tracts of pristine beaches are fantastic for swimming and eager walkers can embark on a 6.5 km scenic walk, taking in various sites associated with the famous Australian aeronautical pioneer, Lawrence Hargrave. Nearby is a picnic area and the **Bullock Track**, the original access route to Illawarra for early settlers. The homely seaside districts of **Thirroul** and **Bulli** are also encountered along the coastal road from Stanwell Park on the way to Wollongong.

Looking north across Bellambi Point, over Wollongong, to Port Kembla beyond.

Bald Hill

Popular with hang-gliders and the spectators of this invigorating pastime, Bald Hill has gained international accolades as a special place for glider activity. The primary take-off point for hang-gliding is Bald Hill at Stanwell Park. A day spent amidst the gliders on the steep hilltops here, overlooking the fringes of Royal National Park, is an event to remember.

The Sydney Hang Gliding Centre (12 Georges Rd, Otford, Ph: 02 4294 4294) has developed a dual-flight "Tandem Training Program" at Stanwell Park, making it possible for an instructor to fly with first-time or inexperienced hang-gliders. The Hang Gliding Centre also flies from "Hill 60" near Port Kembla, just south of Wollongong. Few adrenaline junkies can resist sightseeing from the carriage of a glider as it drifts over the hilltops and coastal seascapes of this dramatically beautiful area.

Lawrence Hargrave Monument, Stanwell Park overlooks the area where the famous aeronautical pioneer conducted much of his work.

Sublime Point Lookout, Illawarra Escarpment This geological wonder has some inspirational views of the area.

Panorama Lookout overlooks South Coast beaches, giving visitors a lasting impression of the region's geographical layout.

Corrimal

Corrimal, to Bulli's south, is an area of historical importance and it retains the Aboriginal name for the region. Today it is a centre for retail, having earned itself the honour of "shopping hub of the north". It was also the preferred home of Henry Kendall, one of Australia's best known 19th-century poets. Today, Corrimal is a lively place with many reminders of its colonial and Indigenous history. A noted Anzac memorial can be found in the town's **Memorial Park**, a quiet and reflective space near the railway station and the Princes Highway.

Thirroul

The **Thirroul** area of Illawarra has a name based on the original Indigenous word for the area, *Thurrural*, meaning "valley of cabbage tree palms". The number of these trees has decreased over the years but groves can still be found in the region. Farming was a common occupation in the area and was followed by a mining boom in the 1860s. A rail link built in the 1880s boosted tourism, attracting Sydney residents to the area. The **Railway Institute Hall**, where Thirroul's workers once studied, has been classified as a heritage building. **Wywurk**, another historic structure in the area, overlooks the sea and was home to famed author D.H. Lawrence, who completed his pastoral/political novel *Kangaroo* here in the 1920s.

Austinmer Surf Life Saving Club has been a landmark of its local beach since 1909.

Coledale

Another scenic showstopper in this coastal region, Coledale is considered to be one of the most attractive areas in all of New South Wales. Its popularity is unsurprising; the stretch of coast from Stanwell Park to Austinmer (including Coledale) has been graded by the Department of Environment and Planning as "a major visual horizon with the highest scenic quality". Previously spelt "Coaldale", the region's name refers to the rich coal deposits of the area. Located on the strip of land between the sea and Illawarra Escarpment, it is 20 km north of Wollongong and its beaches, Coledale and Sharky, are popular spots for swimming.

Coledale Beach is a fantastic surfing location with a camping reserve at the beach's edge.

The starting point for an hour-long walk along Hoddle's Trail starts at the Saddleback Mountain Lookout carpark, which is a 7 km round trip. The track heads west and follows the route trod by surveyor Robert Hoddle in the 1820s. Highlights include a walk-through rainforest and Noorinan Mountain. Half-way along Hoddle's Trail, the path heads south-west through woodland to a spectacular lookout point with vistas south to Foxground and back in the direction of Saddleback. Birdwatching opportunities are also excellent, thanks to a healthy population of resident birdlife.

Kiama Post Office and Harbour

Pilots Cottage Museum, Kiama

The Terrace, Collins Street row of shops.

108

Illawarra and Shoalhaven

To Wollongong's south is the **Shoalhaven** region — a combination of national parks, beaches and rural towns. Highlights from this area include **Kangaroo Valley**, **Seven Mile Beach** and the spectacular **Saddleback Mountain Lookout**. Shellharbour sits on the southern shores of the massive **Lake Illawarra**, and from here it is only 10 km south to pretty **Kiama** along **Shellharbour Road** and the **Princes Highway**. Popular beaches here include **Bombo, Surf Beach** and **Kendall's Beach**.

Between Shellharbour and Kiama

There is much to see and do on the stretch of land between Shellharbour and Kiama. **Bushrangers Bay** at **Bass Point**, 5 km south of Shellharbour on the South Coast, was declared an Aquatic Reserve in 1982 and has become one of the best scuba diving and snorkelling areas in New South Wales. **Killalea State Park**, 90 km south of Sydney, has 8 km of beautiful South Coast coastline, including **Mystics** and **The Farm**, two very popular beaches for surfing and swimming.

Shellharbour A tranquil coastal retreat.

Killalea contains a total of some 250 ha of nature reserve, containing areas of rainforest and picturesque wetlands. Barbecue and picnic areas are also available for visitors. The walks through Killalea's forested areas are particularly attractive. There are also some fine walking tracks passing through sea bird nesting areas and wetlands.

Illawarra Light Rail has steam train and tram rides (open every other Sunday each month, Tongarra Road, Albion Park).

The nearby **Illawarra Light Railway Museum** (Tongarra Rd, Albion Park, north of Kiama, Ph: 02 4256 4627) is another of the area's beloved attractions, offering steam train and tram rides in an appealing retrospective setting. There is an assortment of vintage carriages and steam engines

Kiama Blowhole puts on a show for visitors.

on display in the museum (including the restored *Kiama*, dating back to the early 1900s). The ticket office is built into the original rail terminus of the South Coast railway (designed in the 1800s). On the drive south from Shellharbour, visitors pass the coastal **Cathedral Rocks** site before reaching Kiama. Cathedral Rocks are sea stacks with an eerie resemblance to the spires of a cathedral. This wind- and sea-swept area has intrigued sightseers since the late 19th century. Kiama itself is a picturesque 90 minute drive from Sydney and two hours from Canberra. The Kiama area stretches south to Seven Mile Beach, to Jamberoo Mountain in the west and north to Minnamurra River.

Kiama

Kiama is a lively place with a strong emphasis on outdoor activities. Kiama houses the **Bonaira Native Gardens** (Bonaira Reserve, off Bonaira Street), which has small gardens featuring established rainforest species.

Morton and Budderoo National Parks

For anyone seeking the sheer spectacle of mighty sandstone escarpments, plunging ravines, or towering cliff-faces, Morton and Budderoo National Parks have it all: over 200,000 ha of untamed wilderness, offering visitors a grand range of vertigo-inducing natural wonders.

There is a multitude of impressive plateaus and lookouts from which to observe Morton's and Budderoo's breathtaking expanses. Near Bundanoon, the Echo Point, Grand Canyon and Beauchamp Cliffs vantage points are all accessible by car. From the Hume Highway, both Badgerys and Longpoint Lookouts can be easily reached.

There are a number of superb waterfalls in both parks, cascading deep into rainforested gullies. Belmore Falls (*below left*) and Fitzroy Falls (*right*) are magnificent features of Morton. Carrington Falls (*below centre*) is a popular attraction in Budderoo.

The **Spring Creek Bird Hide** at Kiama's Glenbrook Drive is a birdwatching "hide" that permits up-close and unobstructed views of local waterbirds including thornbills, cormorants and swans.

The **Kiama Blowhole** is an exciting local spectacle, sending towering blasts of water skyward in tune with the surging ocean. **Carrington Falls** is also nearby, displaying a dramatic 50 m waterfall.

At **Blowhole Point** (near the visitors centre) Kiama's maritime and regional museum, the **Pilots Cottage Museum** (Ph: 02 4232 1001), preserves the area's history in a restored cottage staffed by the **Kiama and District Historical Society.**

Another historic housing facility, now known as **The Terrace** (Ph: 02 4232 3322) was built in the 1880s, originally to accommodate Kiama quarrymen. The site now supports a range of tourist-oriented craft and specialty shops and wholesome eateries.

Spring Creek Bird Hide, Spring Creek Wetlands

Mount Pleasant Lookout to Gerringong

Inland Treats

Kiama's inland areas also contain scenic highlights that are worth the visit. Experience nature-based and wilderness activities at the picturesque **Jerrara Dam Arboretum and Wetlands**, situated 5 km west of Kiama on the banks of the dam that once served as Kiama's main water supply. Here visitors will find a pleasant picnic area surrounded by rainforest and freshwater wetlands. South-west of Kiama is the noted **Saddleback Mountain Lookout**. At a towering 600 m above sea-level, the lookout is a prime vantage point for views that take in Sydney's southern beaches to the north and Ulladulla's coast to the south.

The Hampden Suspension Bridge

In 1898, Kangaroo Valley's Hampden Bridge was officially opened. This marvel of colonial engineering celebrated its centenary in 1998. Spanning 77 m, and built from local sandstone, hardwood trusses and steel cable, it is a historic landmark and the only surviving suspension bridge from Australia's colonial days — testimony to the high-quality work performed more than 100 years ago.

Hampden Suspension Bridge, Kangaroo Valley is a timeless relic from Australia's colonial days.

Berry and Nowra

Nowra is situated on the banks of the Shoalhaven River. It is the largest town in the district and an important commercial centre. River tours are a popular diversion as is the Nowra Wildlife Park (Ph: 02 4421 3949). About 20 km north-east of Nowra is the rural township of Berry. Set among lush, undulating hills, boutique wineries and the backdrop of the Cambewarra Range, Berry preserves an elegant sense of history. A good place to discover its rich heritage is at the Gothic-styled Berry Museum (135 Queen St).

Top and above: **Berry** is a beautiful village surrounded by dairy farming land.

Top and above: **Nowra** is the commercial centre of the Shoalhaven region.

Jervis Bay

The vast expanse of **Jervis Bay** laps at the Shoalhaven landscape forging west. Two key areas around Jervis Bay, some 180 km south of Sydney, are **Callala Bay** and **Huskisson**. The southern outskirts and headland areas of Jervis Bay are marked by the 6000 ha **Booderee National Park** and **Sussex Inlet** further south. The coastal road from here leads south to **Ulladulla** and **Mollymook**, eventually leading to the pretty seaside region of the **Clyde Coast**. **Jervis Bay National Park** is also nearby.

Jervis Bay has some of the whitest sands and clearest waters in the world and is frequented by dolphins, whales and myriad invertebrate sea life that are protected within their marine park environment.

Booderee National Park and **Booderee Botanic Gardens** were handed back to the Wreck Bay Aboriginal Community for management in 1995. *Booderee* is an Indigenous word roughly translated as "bay of plenty". Highlights of the park include **Green Patch**, **Bristol Point** and **Cave Beach**, popular sites for weekend retreats.

Jervis Bay National Park

Jervis Bay National Park preserves important plant and animal habitats. One main area of interest is the well-equipped **Greenfield Beach,** with a great selection of picnicking locales and electric barbecue sites. The tranquility of the national park is best experienced in its secluded beaches, coves, bays and forests — all good spots for swimming, bushwalking and birdwatching.

Steamers Beach, Booderee National Park is a glorious, white-sanded escape.

The park's **White Sands Walk**, a round trip along the coast from Greenfield Beach to **Hyams Beach** and back through the **Scribbly Gum Track**, is a perennial park favourite. Well-known picnicking spots include **Hammerhead Point** and **Red Point** near **Callala Bay**, which is on the far northern side of Jervis Bay. Visitor camping is permitted at Booderee, but not at Jervis Bay National Park. **Honeymoon Bay**, on the northern side of the bay, also has camping facilities.

Huskinsson is situated on the clear waters of Jervis Bay and Currrambene Creek.

Jervis Bay National Park Endless stretches of beachside serenity.

Lighthouses of the Region

One of the most intriguing sites around the Jervis Bay region is the ruins of the **Cape St George Lighthouse**, a now-disused lighthouse built in 1860. The location of the lighthouse was ill-considered and almost two dozen ships sank around Jervis Bay's waters in the late 1800s.

In 1889 a new lighthouse was constructed at **Point Perpendicular** and the St George site was used for target practice by the Australian Navy following WWI. Little is now left of the lighthouse, its tower was destroyed and its beacon light used for the **Crookhaven Heads Lighthouse**.

Beecroft Peninsula, a stark and windswept area of jagged cliffs, is another dramatic area of Jervis Bay.

Murrays Beach is a pristine beach with excellent calm-water swimming.

Top: **Bowen Island,** with Murrays Beach and Booderee National Park beyond.
Above: **Point Perpendicular and Point Perpendicular Lighthouse.**

Green Patch Beach is a delightful and safe beach for families.

Local Reminders

At Huskisson, **Lady Denman Museum** (1 Dent St, Huskisson, Ph: 02 4441 5675) houses many reminders and artefacts of the bay's maritime, European and Indigenous history. The site also houses a Sydney ferry, *Lady Denman*, which is undergoing restoration. A "fish pond" of enviable proportions (actually a marine reserve) contains specimens caught by local fishermen, while the **Mangrove Boardwalk** and the **Native Garden** showcase the ecology of this coastal environment.

Green Patch, Booderee National Park where visitors can feed Crimson Rosellas.

Maritime History

The HMAS *Creswell* site (Jervis Bay Road, Jervis Bay, Ph: 02 4429 7900), located on the south-western shores of Jervis Bay in Booderee National Park, was placed on the register of the National Estate by the Australian Heritage Commission in 1981. This served to acknowledge its historical significance and value to present as well as future generations. The site is the Department of Defence's Royal Australian Navy training college.

Nowra, to the north of Jervis Bay, is home to the **Australian Museum of Flight** (Ph: 02 4424 1920) at the HMAS *Albatross* site, on Nowra's Albatross Road. The museum has a large collection of naval aircraft ranging from helicopters to folding-wing aeroplanes and general-purpose aircraft.

Top to bottom: **Timbery's Aboriginal Arts and Crafts; Lady Denman Heritage Complex** Two informative Huskisson attractions.

Common Bronzewing

New Holland Honeyeater

Blue-faced Honeyeater

Satin Bowerbird

Little Penguins

White-bellied Sea Eagle

Wildlife of Jervis Bay and Booderee National Parks

Due to the different environments within their boundaries, these two national parks are home to a wealth of wildlife that inhabits the woodlands, heathlands, rainforest, and coastal regions. Rainforested areas produce a generous assortment of fruit, nectar and insects that possums (Ringtail, Mountain Brushtail and Eastern Pygmy) and gliders (Feathertail, Sugar and Greater) relish.

Swamp Wallabies savour grassy areas of woodland in the park. Long-nosed Potoroos and bandicoots both use the protection of leaf litter and tall grass to conceal themselves during the day, emerging at night to begin foraging in the surface soil.

The rivers and creeks are home to Water Dragons: swift, powerful swimmers that take to water to escape predators and excavate burrows in the soft banks to lay their eggs. Snake-necked Turtles are another common inhabitant in aquatic realms.

Bird species are numerous and thrive in all environments. The Pacific Baza's (*above right*) southernmost range lies within these two parks.

Booderee Botanical Gardens and Walks

With its focus on coastal plants of south-eastern Australia, the Booderee Botanical Gardens comprises some 80 ha of natural bushland and cultivated areas that encircle the dark brown waters of Lake McKenzie.

There are numerous walks throughout the gardens, marked with arrows on wooden posts for ease of exploration. Expect a pleasant mix of regional environments: heathland and rainforest vegetation to dunes and sandstone outcrops. Tread lightly and you can expect to spot Crimson Rosellas, Blue-faced Honeyeaters, New Holland Honeyeaters and the Common Bronzewing pigeon.

Birds of the Sea

Booderee is derived from the Dhurga word meaning "bay of plenty", so it is not surprising that the White-bellied Sea Eagle has forged a comfortable existence around the coast. It is a great predator of marine life, which abounds in this area. This handsome raptor presides as a totem figure over the Aboriginal people of Wreck Bay, and is viewed as a guardian or protector of the area. The beaches also provide perfect habitats for Little Penguins, which breed in rocky cliff-bases and in the dunes.

Birds of the Wetlands

Booderee is a key location for a number of international migratory birds and is also home to some of the most elusive Australian birds. Rarely seen elsewhere, the Eastern Bristlebird is an endangered resident of the swamps and stream thickets of Booderee and can be seen by careful bushwalkers in the Botanical Gardens. Lake McKenzie is home to a number of species of waterfowl, including the Chestnut Teal, White-eyed Duck and Australian Wood Duck.

Birds of the Forests and Woodlands

A multitude of bird species call the woodland areas of these national parks home. Some of the more spectacular avian attractions are the Powerful Owl, the Satin Bowerbird (compulsive collector of trinkets and crafter of one of the most elaborate bowers in the world), and the Superb Lyrebird, master mimic and unashamedly flamboyant suitor.

Southern Spiny Gurnard

Marine Life in Jervis Bay

Jervis Bay Marine Park is a world-renowned conservation area that spans over 100 km of coastline and covers almost 22,000 ha. The park supports many marine habitats (sandy beaches, mangroves, estuaries, sea grass flats, and subtidal and deep reefs) and is a hotbed of marine biodiversity.

Marine life that can be seen from the shore, on boats, or when snorkelling or diving includes Bottlenose Dolphins, Humpback Whales, fur-seals, stingrays, wobbegongs and Port Jackson Sharks, different kinds of seahorses (and their fascinating relative, the Weedy Seadragon) as well as numerous types of soft and hard corals, cone shells, anemones, sponges and sea urchins.

The entire marine park is brimming with weird and wonderful varieties of fish, including wrasse, pigfishes, goatfishes, seaperches and lionfishes, all of which make their homes around Jervis Bay's subtidal reefs.

Bluestriped Goatfish

Port Jackson Shark

Sea Anemone

Cone Shell

Bigbelly Seahorse

Marine Life Outside Jervis Bay — The Deep Reefs

Comb Wrasse

The outer reefs of Jervis Bay Marine Park contain some spectacular diving and fishing locations. The area has powerful currents and steep, shelving drop-offs, as well as many different varieties of marine life not likely to be encountered closer to shore.

A number of pelagic species frequent these environs and attract recreational anglers from all around the world. The fishes targeted include Yellowtail Kingfish, marlin, and tuna. On the reefs Nannygais, Giant Boarfish, and John Dory are among the most prized catches.

Roughy

The deep, temperate waters contain impressive underwater caves and rock formations. The labyrinth of nooks, crannies and underwater lairs hide canny and secretive fish species, such as the Eastern Blue Groper — once overfished but now fully protected in New South Wales.

One of the rarest and most unusual visitors to this area is the Mola Mola or Oceanic Sunfish. These gentle behemoths are truly awesome creatures: growing to over 3 m in length and weighing more than 2000 kg, Sunfish will visit "cleaning stations" in the area, where cleanerfishes remove parasites that attach themselves to the Sunfish's gills and mouth.

Banded Seaperch

Pigfish

Seawhip Anemone

School of Hussar

Halfbanded Seaperch

Eastern Blue Devil

Eastern Blue Groper

Giant Boarfish

Milton Ulladulla Historical Society's oldest house, dating from 1850.

Warden Head (Lighthouse) and the South Pacific Heathland Reserve

Situated south of Ulladulla harbour, the South Pacific Heathland Reserve is a good walking area with safe tracks and educational information about the reserve's plentiful flora and fauna. Lookouts permit views of birdlife, including Yellow-Tailed Black Cockatoos and New Holland Honeyeaters, in their natural habitat. There are also great views of the area's pristine coastline.

From here walkers reach the old lighthouse at Warden Head, heading north along the beach at low tide and around the promontory. Crafted from curved, wrought iron plates, the lighthouse originated in an Ulladulla foundry in 1873 and was moved to its present site in 1879.

Warden Head is a popular spot for rock fishing and has pleasant views of the harbour and its surrounding environs.

Top to bottom: Bawley Point; Kioloa has pleasant scenery, rocky headlands and quiet beaches.

114

Clyde Coast

The picturesque **Clyde Coast** region of the New South Wales South Coast stretches from **Ulladulla** to **Batemans Bay**. The main road heading south is the coastal Princes Highway, passing the popular tourism spots of **Lake Tabourie** and **Bawley Point**.

A short drive south of Ulladulla is **Burrill Lake**, a popular waterway lending itself to a variety of leisure pursuits including swimming, canoeing, windsurfing, fishing and water-skiing. Natural landmarks around the lake include **Kings Point** and **Dolphin Point**, ideal for picnicking or just kicking back and savouring the sights.

Top to bottom: **Mollymook; Ulladulla** These neighbouring towns will delight visitors who are looking for a special coastal holiday with a large range of recreational activities, accommodation and superb surf breaks.

Lakes and Their Beaches

The lakes in the area are fringed with a series of long, untouched beaches stretching far along the northern **Clyde Coast — Wairo, Tabourie, Meroo, Racecourse, Merry** and **Pretty Beaches** feature pristine white sands and plenty of solitude for those who enjoy long, uninterrupted shoreline strolls. **Lake Tabourie**, just over 10 km south of Ulladulla, has a well-appointed museum featuring examples of local fauna, Aboriginal and European history, and period pieces illustrating the region's history. The peaceful breezes and quiet villages of the region make for a delightful weekend getaway.

A Pigeon's House on a Mountain?

Presiding inland is **Pigeon House Mountain**, named by naval explorer James Cook in the 1770s who recorded that it "resembles a square dovehouse with a dome on top and for that reason I named it Pigeon House." It was originally known to local Aboriginals as *Didhol*. Located in **Morton National Park**, south-west of Ulladulla and an hour north-west from Batemans Bay, Pigeon House Mountain forms part of the escarpment dividing the coastal plain from the interior tableland.

Aboriginal bora grounds, Morton National Park has magnificent views of the distant Pigeon House Mountain.

Burril Lake is situated just 5 km south of Ulladulla and is fringed by native bushland.

Close to Pigeon House Mountain, the **Shrouded Gods Mountain** and **Byangee Walls** landmarks can also be spotted. The climb to the summit of Pigeon House Mountain, which rises some 700 m above sea level, is accessible for energetic hikers. The mountain's peak promises a superb 360° panoramic view, displaying ocean, national park and river scenery. The access road to the start of the mountain climb passes through areas of old eucalypt forest.

Budawang National Park

There are many notable and sometimes quite remote landmarks in the area of **Budawang National Park**, adjoining the southern end of **Morton National Park**, and the Upper Clyde area. These require a bit more effort but are definitely worthwhile. Budawang is noted for its spectacular and mountainous **Scenic Rim**, a cliff-line topped by views of the local landmarks of Pigeon House Mountain, **Corang Peak** and **The Castle** (which is considered by some to be even more spectacular than Pigeon House). The rugged and hilly country encountered here only enhances the wide, sweeping coastal views seen to east. Climbs to the summit of The Castle are also possible, although much more arduous than those to the peak of Pigeon House.

On the ocean coast, further south of Bawley Point, lies **Pebbly Beach** and **Murramarang National Park.** The Clyde River and the southern end of Budawang National Park lie to the north-west. The Kings Highway heads north-west, crossing the Clyde River and passing the towns of **Nelligen** and **Braidwood** and the southern tip of Budawang, before heading towards Canberra.

Budawang National Park

Clockwise from top left: Common Wombat; Swamp Wallaby; Greater Glider.

Approximately 50 km west of Ulladulla lies Budawang National Park. Budawang is a particularly rugged and remote region — the majority of this national park is a declared wilderness area, therefore vehicular access is limited.

For accomplished and hardy trekkers, Budawang provides a serious bushwalking experience into unforgiving and unforgettable country. The park is a mixture of ironwood and temperate rainforest that is a sanctuary for marsupial species, including the Swamp Wallaby and the Common Wombat, as well as the elusive Greater Glider. The summit of Mt Budawang is a worthy challenge giving views of Southern Highlands that are nothing short of sensational. Walkers should carry reliable equipment and adequate food and water, and be prepared for isolated conditions.

Batemans Bay at sunrise.

The Buckenbowra "Corn Trail" Walk

The 12 km Corn Trail track through Buckenbowra State Forest is a challenging half-day activity. The trail was first used in the 1830s to facilitate trade with the Southern Tablelands. The goods were transported along the track on pack-horses. Clyde Mountain, 35 km from Batemans Bay along the Kings Highway route to Braidwood, marks the start of the walk. The track traverses a large area of eucalypt forest to the Bolero Valley. The climb is steep in places but provides inspiring views of the mountain-top cloaked atmospherically in mist.

Batemans Bay

As the Princes Highway heads south from the northern points of the Clyde Coast it passes the beautiful **Pebbly Beach** and **Murramarang National Park** on its way to spectacular **Batemans Bay.** From Batemans Bay the Kings Highway heads inland, crossing the Clyde River before heading north-west to the **Southern Highlands** and **Canberra.**

The wide waterway at Batemans Bay is at the mouth of the Clyde River, 280 km south of Sydney. First noticed, and named, by James Cook in 1770, the bay is the largest on the New South Wales South Coast. Despite its size, the area has managed to retain a friendly village-like feel. It bears the name of Nathaniel Bateman, fellow seaman and colleague of (soon to be Captain) James Cook.

The Bay's History

In 1797, survivors from the wreck of the ship *Sydney Cove* were stranded in the area and are thought to be the first Europeans to discover Batemans Bay. Only a handful survived the long and arduous journey back to Sydney. Later that year, George Bass ventured south, arriving in Batemans Bay in December of 1797.

Bass, born in 1771 and raised in Lincolnshire, England, was a Royal Navy surgeon. He served aboard several ships before being appointed to HMS *Reliance,* which sailed for New South Wales in 1795.

After arrival in Sydney, he explored the **Georges River** and in 1796 he set out to explore the New South Wales South Coast, reaching **Lake Illawarra.** The following year Bass returned to the South Coast to obtain specimens and, at the same time, he also confirmed the discovery of coal deposits at **Coalcliff.**

Batemans Bay was visited regularly during the 1820s and 1830s. In the 1850s, James McCauley, a pioneer settler, journeyed to **Nelligen** along the Clyde River, and soon a major road from Nelligen to the goldfields at **Braidwood** (north-west of Nelligen and Batemans Bay) was completed in 1856. This gave cause for a permanent township at Batemans Bay to be laid out in 1859.

It was only a small township with a population of 200; however, in 1892 (when gold was discovered in Batemans Bay) this figure increased rapidly.

The Bay Today

Today, a visit to Batemans Bay should include a visit to the town of Nelligen, 10 km upstream on a quiet stretch of the picturesque Clyde River. River cruises are a great way to view the region and are available through several boating companies in Batemans Bay. Try **Boatshed Merinda** (Ph: 02 4472 4052), **Clyde River Cruises** (Ph: 02 4478 1005) or Moruya Aero Club, Batemans Bay (Ph: 02 4472 8044).

Swimming, boardriding, diving, snorkelling, fishing, sailing and windsurfing are other popular activities in the region.

There are also many interesting terrestrial attractions surrounding Batemans Bay, including the **Clyde River and Batemans Bay Historical Society Museum** (1 Museum Place, Batemans Bay, Ph: 02 4472 8993, open Thursdays and Saturdays from 1.00 p.m. – 4.00 p.m.), which houses much local history and a diverse collection of regional artefacts and photographs.

Left, top and bottom: **Bateman's Bay** has a small town atmosphere and a fabulous estuary location.

Wondrous Wildlife

The **Birdland Animal Park** (55 Beach Road, Ph: 02 4472 5364) provides refuge for a number of animals, including wombats and snakes brought out each day for crowd-pleasing public handling sessions. There are also nurseries, ponds and exploratory rides through the park aboard the *Birdsville Express* train. Another wildlife highlight of the area is the ideal opportunity presented in the **Durras** region, 17 km north of Batemans Bay. This popular holiday resort area, on the edge of **Murramarang National Park,** is readily accessed from the Princes Highway. Durras gives visitors the opportunity to get up-close-and-personal with the mob of kangaroos that inhabit the local beach. It has little tourist development, and is ideal for those who wish to enjoy the natural beauty of the region and its bushwalking, swimming and fishing activities.

Mogo

The township of **Mogo**, situated 10 km south-west of Batemans Bay, is also well worth an exploratory visit. Its quaint and rustic setting is enhanced by antique shops and vintage buildings. Mogo was born during the region's gold rush in the 1800s and the **Old Mogo Town Gold Rush Theme Park** (Ph: 02 4474 2123) takes modern-day visitors back to Mogo's gold rush heyday. There are opportunities to visit a mine tunnel or fossick for gold.

One particular highlight is the **Mogo Zoo** (22 Tomakin Rd, Ph: 02 4474 4930), a fascinating sanctuary for over 100 animals, including dozens of rare species.

Braidwood Gold

When gold fever broke out in the Araluen Valley during 1851, the majority of fossickers descended on Braidwood, the historic town 60 km north-west of Batemans Bay. Braidwood's population exploded when gold digging commenced as thousands of people flocked to the area, including Sydney's first tea baron, Quong Tart. Gold also seduced society's more nefarious characters. The legendary bushranger Ben Hall and the famous Clarke gang plied their dubious trade around Braidwood. A 170 kilogram nugget, unearthed in 1869, holds the record as Braidwood's most impressive discovery.

Murramarang National Park

A 40 km drive north of Batemans Bay leads to Murramarang National Park, a real gem in this sparkling region, with its incredible beaches, gorgeous lakes, and outstanding views both up and down the coast. The park is home to impressive forests of native Spotted Gum, some of the largest in New South Wales. The park's most popular attraction is Pebbly Beach (*below*), where Eastern Grey Kangaroos lead a leisurely existence pampered by visiting tourists.

Bottlenose Dolphins

The Murramarang Aboriginal Area is a place of spiritual significance. It contains a number of burial sites and perhaps the largest midden pile on the South Coast — several hectares of stone artefacts and scattered deposits (shellfish as well as the bones of fishes and small mammals) from various tribes who lived in the area up to 12,000 years ago. The plants, animals, land and waterways all have spiritual relevance to the Indigenous people of Murramarang.

Batemans Bay is the ideal departure point for scenic drives, elevated panoramic viewing and bushwalking treks as the area is surrounded by several State forests, including those of **Mogo, Boyne, Benandarah,** and **Buckenbowra.** The region has a number of superb lookouts and vantage points from which to survey the area. **Batemans Bay's Observation Point,** has good views of Batemans Bay, overlooking other local landmarks such as **North Head** and **Malua Bay.** Towards the south is **Round Hill Fire Tower Lookout** on the Princes Highway, 2 km south of Batemans Bay. The **Batemans Bay Tourist Information Centre** (corner of the Princes Highway and Beach Road, Batemans Bay, Ph: 02 4472 6900 or freecall 1800 802 528) has details on all attractions for visitors to the area.

Pretty Beach in Murramarang National Park.

Canberra is the capital city of Australia, located in the north of the Australian Capital Territory, or ACT. It has a population of around 325,000 and is the country's largest inland city. Through a quirk of national history, Canberra was diplomatically placed between Melbourne and Sydney to quell an inter-city feud regarding which city should be the nation's political capital. Situated 280 km from Sydney and 660 km from Melbourne, Canberra now attracts many visitors who travel to the national capital to appreciate the world-class exhibits on display in the city's prestigious galleries and museums.

Gang-gang Cockatoo

Canberra — The Nation's Capital

Canberra lies beneath the north-eastern slopes of the Australian Alps on the ancient lands of the Ngunnawal Aboriginal people and its name comes from the Aboriginal word meaning "meeting place". Settlers first visited the Canberra region in the 1830s and it was selected as the national capital early in 1908. It is somewhat unique among Australian capital cities, being an entirely purpose-built and fully "customised" city. As a result, modern-day Canberra now possesses a tidy, linear and orderly appearance, rather unlike Australia's State capitals, which have undergone a more sporadic, rambling evolution.

From the outset, Canberra was designed to be beautiful — its appearance was influenced by Walter Burley Griffin, an American architect and designer from Chicago, whose winning entry in the "Federal Capital Design Competition" trumped the other 137 aspiring entrants. The original sketches and plans, which Burley Griffin submitted on cotton cloth, remain in the **National Archives of Australia** to this day.

The Commonwealth Parliament has only occupied three buildings throughout Australia's history. Australia's first parliament met in Melbourne when the Commonwealth of Australia was formed (in 1901) and there was no federal capital. A temporary Provisional Parliament Building (now known as **Old Parliament House**) was opened in Canberra in 1927. In 1988, the **New Parliament House** was opened as Australia's seat of government. Its distinctive centrepiece, a towering flagpole, became an instantly recognisable icon around the nation.

Canberra also houses the **High Court of Australia**, the seat of Australia's highest court of appeal, which contains three courtrooms and a seven-storey public hall as well as other government departments and the embassies of many foreign nations. In addition, it is home to many of Australia's social and cultural institutions.

Some larger regional centres surrounding Canberra include **Yass**, **Queanbeyan** and **Wagga Wagga**. To its south-west are the **Snowy River**, **Cooma,** the ski resorts of **Thredbo, Perisher Valley, Smiggins** and **Jindabyne**, and the rugged **Kosciuszko National Park**.

Top to bottom: **Captain Cook Memorial Water Jet; The National Carillon; The High Court of Australia; National Capital Exhibition.**

Australian War Memorial, Canberra

Australian Institute of Sport

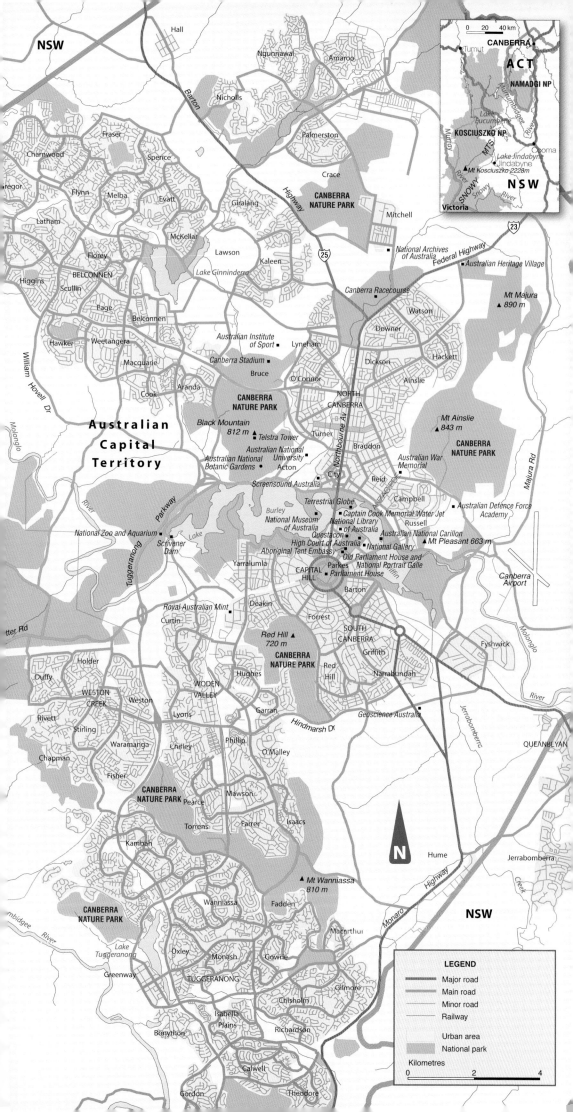

Top to bottom: **Terrestrial Globe; Commonwealth Park** Features of Lake Burley Griffin.

The Australian Institute of Sport Base camp for the country's premier athletes.

The Australian Institute of Sport
Known simply as the AIS or "The Institute" (Leverrier Crescent, Bruce, ACT, Ph: 02 6214 1111), this facility for elite sportsmen/women is well worth a visit. Since 1981, the AIS has been at the forefront of sports science and has helped orchestrate the world-beating performances of Australian athletes in more than 25 different sports.

Canberra

The collection of museums, galleries and other attractions that dot the Canberra landscape are truly befitting of a national capital. Amid the tidy landscape of this city are some of the country's most revered works of art, cultural vantage points and monuments to history. A grand panorama of many of these major cultural, political or historical buildings can be enjoyed from Lake Burley Griffin.

Lake Burley Griffin

Perhaps one of the most attractive spots to begin an exploration of the Australian capital is on the shores of **Lake Burley Griffin**, built in 1963 after the **Molonglo River** was dammed, and named in honour of the city's designer. The lake is about 11 km long, a little over a kilometre wide at its widest point and has 40 km of shoreline and six islands. The 33 m tall **Scrivener Dam** regulates the lake's flow.

To some, Lake Burley Griffin is the true centerpiece of Canberra. The lake and its manicured surrounds are extremely picturesque and comprise the geographical centre of Canberra as per the original plans of Walter Burley Griffin.

Swimming in Lake Burley Griffin's waters is rare, although boating and rowing are common pastimes. Fishing, cycling, jogging and barbecues are also popular activities along the lake's shoreline, especially in summer.

Blundell's Cottage was built in 1858 by pioneer Robert Campbell and features artefacts from the 19th century.

One of the lake's larger islands is **Aspen Island**, connected to dry land by a footbridge. It is also the site of the **Australian National Carillon,** an immense 55-bell bell tower that was given to the Australian people by the British Government to commemorate the 50th anniversary of Canberra as the nation's capital. It was officially opened by the Queen in 1970.

Duntroon House, also built by Robert Campbell, is now the officer's mess at the Royal Military College.

Lakeside homage is also paid to Captain James Cook in the form of a memorial. This memorial is made up of the **Terrestrial Globe**, which tells the story of Cook's three major seafaring adventures, and the **Captain Cook Memorial Jet**, a massive jet that shoots plumes of water 150 m into the air. The jet was officially inaugurated in 1970 by Queen Elizabeth II to commemorate the bicentenary of Cook's first sighting of Australia's east coast.

Yarralumla is the Governor-General's beautiful residence, previously an early pioneering family's homestead.

Of Historical Interest

There are many places of historical interest in and around Canberra, thanks to the area's rich Indigenous and farming heritage. Visitors can visit **Duntroon House, Yarralumla, Lanyon Homestead** and **Blundell's Cottage** — all lovingly restored homes capturing the essence of 19th-century life.

Lanyon Homestead is a grazing property from the 19th century situated on the banks of Murrumbidgee River.

Above, left to right: **Old Parliament House** is now a museum and contains the National Portrait Gallery and exhibitions; **The view through the Great Verandah, New Parliament House** Designed by American-based architects Mitchell/Giurgola and Thorp, Parliament House is surrounded by 23 ha of landscaped gardens that are open daily for leisurely walks.

Above, left and right: **The bold geometric interior of Parliament House; The Young Citizen Quilt** at the National Capital Exhibition at Regatta Point tells the story of how Canberra was named, designed and built. Visitors can also learn about the Indigenous people of Canberra and their fascinating link with the Bogong Moth.

Telstra Tower

Perhaps one of the best places to survey the lake from is **Telstra Tower** (Black Mountain Drive, Acton, Canberra, Ph: 02 6219 6111), rising almost 200 m above the surrounding scenery. It has a number of functional roles: one as Canberra's unofficial "compass" (visitors keep it in sight to maintain their bearings), and another as a state-of-the-art telecommunications centre. It is also an excellent observation post. It has two open-air viewing platforms and an enclosed viewing area for 360° panoramic sightseeing.

Telstra Tower is a distinctive Canberra landmark and popular tourist attraction.

The tower also houses its own telecommunications museum, café, gift shop, and revolving restaurant, serving superb food and offering the best views in the city. In 1989 the World Federation of Great Towers admitted Telstra Tower into a select group of noted architectural structures, which includes London's Blackpool Tower and New York's Empire State Building. It has become one of Canberra's most noted and recognisable attractions and is open to the public every day from 9 a.m. – 10 p.m.

Parliament House, opened in 1988, sits above Old Parliament House and stands on Capital Hill. The curved granite walls embrace 4500 rooms surmounted by an 81 m stainless steel flagpole flying the huge Australian flag. This showcase of Australian stone and timber took a workforce of 10,000 more than eight years to complete.

Anzac Parade

One of the finest and most spectacular thoroughfares in all of Australia is the immense **Anzac Parade**. Opened in 1965 to coincide with the 50th anniversary of the ANZAC landing in Gallipoli, its distinctive red gravel walkway escorts the eye down to **New Parliament House** from the **Australian War Memorial (AWM)**. As the national capital's major ceremonial avenue, it is set along the magnificent land axis that forms a key feature of the original plan for Canberra designed by Walter Burley Griffin. Anzac Parade is easily distinguishable, especially when viewed from **Mount Ainslie**.

Top to bottom: **Anzac Parade; Entrance to the Australian War Memorial** Together these are two of Canberra's most recognisable landmarks and form a solemn setting for many of the country's most important military commemorations.

Ten memorials decorate the parade, including the **Australian Army Memorial**, the **Australian Vietnam Forces National Memorial** and the intriguing **Rats of Tobruk Memorial**. The parade is crowned at each end by two of the country's most noted buildings, namely Parliament House and the Australian War Memorial: the latter being one of the world's greatest museums (Treloar Crescent, Campbell, Ph: 02 6243 4211). The Australian War Memorial has amassed a vital collection of wartime artefacts and historical pieces over the last century. Holdings include official and private records and logs, photographs, heraldry, military technology and family histories relating to Australian servicemen and women.

Australia on Display

The **National Museum of Australia** (Lawson Crescent, Acton Peninsula, Ph: 02 6208 5000), which opened in 2001, allows visitors the opportunity to explore what it means to be Australian. With themes concentrating on Australia's past and future and hands-on activities that will appeal to children and adults, it showcases a huge collection ranging from a preserved Thylacine, the extinct Tasmania Tiger, to genuine convict clothing.

For technology and science buffs, **Questacon** (King Edward Terrace, Ph: 1800 020 603) takes its visitors on a fascinating journey of discovery, with exhibits that bring the physical world and its natural phenomena within reach of inquisitive minds. Or, examine a 150-million-year-old dinosaur shin bone and learn about the history of life on Earth through a series of fossil replicas at the **National Dinosaur Museum** (Gold Creek Village, Ph: 1800 356 000).

Canberra's art galleries, such as the **National Gallery of Australia** (Parkes Place, Parkes, Ph: 02 6240 6504), display examples of the world's best art from a number of important periods. The **National Library of Australia** (Parkes Place, Ph: 02 6262 1111) has over three million books to enthral bookworms, historians and art lovers.

The National Dinosaur Museum, with over 300 exhibits, including replica dinosaur skeletons and life-size reconstructions of a number of Australian Dinosaurs will fascinate visitors.

Questacon demonstrates the impact of science and technology on everyday life though entertaining, interactive displays. Visitors can get close to a lightning bolt, experience an earthquake or freefall 6 m down a vertical slide, emerging unscathed.

National Museum of Australia The museum building itself is monumental and compelling, surrounding a surreal outdoor courtyard called the Garden of Australian Dreams. Inside are many wonderful exhibitions.

Tidbinbilla — Sanctuary and Space Station

A 40 minute drive from Canberra's city centre, Tidbinbilla Nature Reserve is a scenic valley lying between the Tidbinbilla and Gibraltar Ranges. Together with Namadgi National Park, Tidbinbilla forms the northern section of the Australian Alps. The area also represents a harmonious, albeit curious, union of rich cultural heritage, natural beauty, and modern technological development.

The mountains surrounding *Tidbinbilla* (derived from an Aboriginal word for "a place where boys become men") contain a number of Indigenous artefacts and rock shelters. Visitors will also notice the reserve's 160-year-old European influence in pioneering houses and other scattered remnants from the area's colonial past.

The Canberra Deep Space Communication Complex (*left*) is another feature of Tidbinbilla. As one of the integral sites of NASA's Deep Space Network, the complex is part of an international network of antennas supporting exploration and scientific research throughout the cosmos.

Visitors can see displays and obtain information about Tidbinbilla Nature Reserve's features, history, guided walks and other activities from the visitor centre.

Top to bottom: Eastern Grey Kangaroos cavorting on the lawns at the Deep Space Communication Complex; Tidbinbilla Nature Reserve Visitor Centre.

The **National Archives of Australia** (Queen Victoria Terrace, Parkes, Ph: 02 6212 3900) also has significant holdings, primarily those relating to Australian government and officialdom after Federation in 1901. Its record-keeping helps make the Australian Government accountable to its public by tracing the history of major political decisions and events. Unlike the kind of literature found at most public libraries, the archive holdings tend to be of an official, government-oriented nature. There are plans, photos, maps, architectural drawings, films, even sound recordings, scripts and musical scores.

Parks and Gardens

Mount Ainslie, behind the AWM and accessed via walking tracks at the rear of the building, is an excellent high point overlooking Canberra and gives a splendid view straight down Anzac Parade to Lake Burley Griffin and New Parliament House beyond. It provides an ideal aspect for examining the city's land axis: a key feature of Griffin's original plan linking Capital Hill and Mt Ainslie. Lake Burley Griffin and the mountain ranges that surround the city are also visible from here and the views of Parliament, Anzac Parade and the AWM are exceptional.

Another ideal lookout is **Black Mountain**, home to Telstra Tower. The mountain has a series of attractive walks and at its foot is the site of the **Australian National Botanic Gardens** (Ph: 02 6250 9540). The Botanic Gardens focus on native plants and contain one of the country's best collections of Australian flora. Highlights of the gardens are the climatic zones designed to replicate the actual environment of specific plant habitats — desert, rainforest, and mountain. Trails follow the landscaped **Rainforest Gully, Eucalypt Garden, Rock Garden** and **Mallee Shrublands**.

The **Tulip Top Gardens** on the Federal Highway outside Canberra (Ph: 02 6230 3077) is another botanical wonderland that will appeal to visitors seeking out the area's more peaceful places.

Left to right: Australian National Botanic Gardens; relaxing by Lake Burley Griffin; Spring tulips.

Index

Index

The Sydney Opera House is the single most photographed building in Australia. It is a challenge for most photographers, all of whom attempt to capture its grandeur in a frame a little different from anyone else's.

Acknowledgements

Photography: Steve Parish

Photographic assistance: Emma Harm, Catherine Prentice & Phillip Hayson.

Additional photography: p. 8, George St, Sydney 1908, courtesy of Historic Photographs www.historicphotographs.com.au; p. 9 Women's athletics, Olympic Games 2000, Emma Harm; p. 12 Sydney Gay and Lesbian Mardi Gras, City to Surf, both by Robert James Wallace; p. 13 Telstra Stadium, Robert James Wallace; p. 29 Poppies in the Royal Botanic Gardens (bottom right), Emma Harm; p. 61 Galah (top left), Ken Stepnell; p. 64 Aboriginal rock art on the Resolute Track (top), Allan Fox; p. 64 Beach in Ku-ring-gai National Park (bottom), Allan Fox; p. 65 Bushland, Ku-ring-gai National Park (top), Allan Fox; p. 65 Spotted-tailed Quoll (bottom left), Ken Stepnell; p. 68 Rouse Hill Estate (top left), Courtesy of Historic Houses Trust; p. 71 Green and Golden Bell Frog (top left) Ian Morris; p. 74 Red-bellied Black Snake, Red-crowned Toadlet, Pobblebonk Frog, all by Ian Morris; p. 87 Wollemi pine, Courtesy of Neilson's Native Nursery, Brisbane; p. 88 Tanilba House, Courtesy of Historic Tanilba House; p. 102 Fig Tree Cave, Wombeyan Caves, http://en.wikipedia.org/wiki/Image:Wombeyan_Caves_Fig_Tree_Cave_Interior.jpg; p. 102, Cricketers playing outside the Bradman Museum, Bowral (bottom left), Courtesy of the Bradman Foundation; p. 102 The Old Bakery Cottage, Berrima (bottom right), Lees Lizards Photography; p. 112 New Holland Honeyeater, Blue-faced Honeyeater and Satin Bowerbird, all by Ken Stepnell; p. 112 Pacific Baza (top right), Peter Slater; p. 115 Pigeon House Mountain & Aboriginal Bora Grounds in foreground (top left), Allan Fox.

Text: Robert James Wallace; Ted Lewis, SPP; Michele Perry, SPP
Series design: Leanne Nobilio, SPP
Finished art: Leanne Nobilio, SPP
Editorial: Michele Perry, SPP; Ted Lewis, SPP; Karin Cox, SPP
Production: Tiffany Johnson, SPP
Maps supplied by MAPgraphics, Brisbane, Australia
Prepress by Colour Chiefs Digital Imaging, Brisbane, Australia
Printed in China by PrintPlus Ltd

Published by Steve Parish Publishing Pty Ltd
PO Box 1058, Archerfield, Queensland 4108 Australia

www.steveparish.com.au

© copyright Steve Parish Publishing Pty Ltd

ISBN 174021924 4
10 9 8 7 6 5 4 3 2 1

online

FOR PRODUCTS
www.steveparish.com.au

FOR LIMITED EDITION PRINTS
www.steveparishexhibits.com.au

FOR PHOTOGRAPHY EZINE
www.photographaustralia.com.au